BUILT to LAST

Outdoor
FURNITURE

BUILT to LAST

Outdoor
FURNITURE

14 TIMELESS WOODWORKING PROJECTS
FOR THE YARD, DECK, AND PATIO

By the Editors at Skills Institute Press

skills institute press

Distributed By
Fox Chapel Publishing

FOX CHAPEL
PUBLISHING

© 2011 by Skills Institute Press LLC
"Built to Last" series trademark of Skills Institute Press
Published and distributed in North America by Fox Chapel Publishing Company, Inc.

Outdoor Furniture is an original work, first published in 2011.

Portions of text and art previously published by and reproduced under license with Direct Holdings Americas Inc.

ISBN 978-1-56523-500-7

Library of Congress Cataloging-in-Publication Data

Outdoor furniture.
    p. cm. -- (Built to last)
Includes index.
ISBN 978-1-56523-500-7
1. Outdoor furniture. 2. Furniture making. I. Fox Chapel Publishing.
TT197.5.O9O982 2010
684.1'8--dc22
                                    2010033919

To learn more about the other great books from Fox Chapel Publishing,
or to find a retailer near you, call toll-free 800-457-9112 or visit us at
www.FoxChapelPublishing.com.

Note to Authors: We are always looking for talented authors to write new books
in our area of woodworking, design, and related crafts.
Please send a brief letter describing your idea to
Acquisition Editor, 1970 Broad Street, East Petersburg, PA 17520.

Printed in China
First printing: April 2011

Contents

What You Can Learn

Facing the Elements, page 16

By the nature of where it spends its life, outdoor furniture has to be designed, first and foremost, to withstand its toughest enemy — the elements.

Chairs, page 24

Outdoor furniture must be designed to rough it, and the Adirondack chair, chaise longue, and curved chair featured here are all up to the task.

Benches, page 56

Benches invite company, so here are three different styles with complete building instructions.

Tables, page 80

The patio table and the folding picnic table are excellent additions to any outdoor furniture ensemble.

Swings and Gliders, page 104

Pleasant and relaxing, a swing or gliding settee provides an ideal accessory to a porch or garden as well as offering interesting mechanical challenges to the home woodworker.

Garden Projects, page 120

The arbor, planter, and serving trolley presented in this chapter complement the furniture designs featured elsewhere in this book.

A Gallery of Outdoor Furniture Designs

Adirondack chair
(page 26)

Bench with gliding base
(page 114)

Garden bench
(page 58)

Curved chair
(page 36)

Keyed-tenon bench
(page 100)

Chaise longue
(page 46)

Park bench
(page 66)

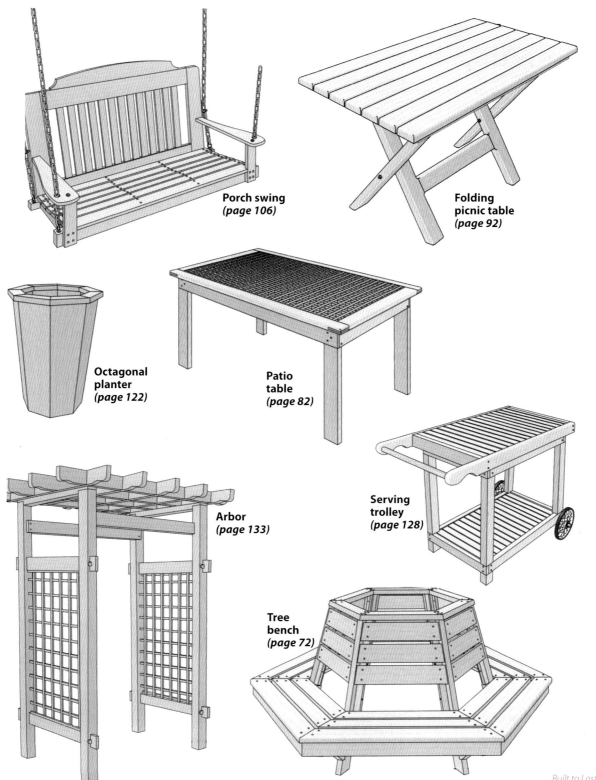

Porch swing
(page 106)

**Folding
picnic table**
(page 92)

**Octagonal
planter**
(page 122)

**Patio
table**
(page 82)

Arbor
(page 133)

**Serving
trolley**
(page 128)

**Tree
bench**
(page 72)

A Gallery of Outdoor Furniture Designs

Long-Lasting Furniture

I'm going to do *what* to that lovely chair and table set? Well, I intend to expose it to the direct heat and ultraviolet rays of the sun. Then I'll let it get soaking wet, freeze, and then thaw out with blasts of warm, dry air. And I'm going to allow this to happen not just once, but over and over again for the next two to three decades. Well, of course I am: I'm building a piece of outdoor furniture.

The question is, how can I possibly build wood furniture to endure such horrific abuse? To find some answers, I looked back to the principles and practices of the carriage and boat builders of the last century. It was, after all, these tradesmen who produced some of the most highly stressed and severely exposed—not to mention beautiful—structures known to man. If these trades could do that, I was betting they could build one heck of a lawn chair.

What I learned boiled down to this: These craftsmen asked much of every piece of wood that went into a ship or carriage, but they never asked more that it could give—and they did all they could to preserve its integrity. They chose woods that were inherently rot-resistant, being careful not to include sapwood, splits, pitch pockets, cross-grain, or other defects that might diminish its strength or longevity.

They cut the exposed shoulders of joints at water-shedding angles and applied bedding compounds like pine tar and Irish felt to the mating surfaces—strategies that helped prevent moisture from intruding, lingering, and nourishing wood-eating parasites. They designed channels, drain holes, and dams throughout the structure to encourage water to flow away from the wood. They avoided flat surfaces, bowing the tops of horizontal areas like rails and box lids to discourage puddling. And where fasteners were needed (though they minimized their use as much as possible by using wood wedges and pins), they chose metals that resisted rust and were not corrosive to the wood.

While I don't intend to build America while sitting in my lawn furniture (I don't even intend to be awake), I do want the fruits of my labors to serve my family for many years. To that end I employ much of what I have learned from these long-gone tradesmen. And, so far, that chair and table have remained lovely, continuing to do the job for which they were intended—while living happily outdoors.

- Jim Tolpin

A builder of outdoor furniture and boats, Jim Tolpin is also author of several books about woodworking and furniture making. He lives in Port Townsend, Washington. He is shown here inside a tinker's wagon that he built many years ago from Douglas-fir and tongue-and-groove pine.

Rustic Furniture

Trees have been my neighbors for a quarter century. My book on rustic furniture, a dozen years in the making and essentially about "tree art," was researched and written within the Adirondack forest, in a clearing of the museum grounds that was home to me and my family for 20 years. Our next home, where I write this, is *in* the woods. Doe and fawn, vixen and pup, have made their careful way through the mixed forest and its tender undergrowth of moss, ferns, and wildflowers, unaware of my spying on them from my study window. On clear days, the sun glints on Long Lake, relieving the sultry shadows in which the house is usually cast.

The Adirondacks have many features that make the area an incomparable natural treasure. People play in its waters, climb its mountains, seek its solitude, and search out the wildlife that roam the forest. For me, the Adirondack forest reigns supreme. Nearly unbroken and extending roughly a hundred miles north to south, the forest nurtures all that swims, crawls, and flies. The forest has shaped the region's culture and does so even today. Once, thousands of men and women worked in the forest, cutting its trees while living in crude log shanties miles from home, family, or any real town. Today, although logging occupies far fewer people, it remains an important Adirondack industry—and the forest a dominant presence in residents' lives, shaping a culture that is different and distinct from rural cultures elsewhere.

That outdoor furniture, especially of the twiggy kind, should be a product of this forest environment is not surprising. What more natural furnishings should spring from the forest? Perhaps more surprising is the style's popularity among urbanites. It was a craft that was practised nearly everywhere in the American East between 1825 and 1900. Rustic benches and garden houses were assembled in Manhattan and shipped wherever there was a buyer and conveyance. The resurgence that began in the early 1970s continues, to my pleasant surprise, to this day.

This rustic craft jogs a memory made of our arboreal heritage among the builders and buyers. Who knows why someone purchases a chair of branches and roots for an apartment 30 floors off the pavement? In any event, that lonely chair, a talisman of nature in the city, can perform its therapy as long as there are forests to visit and dream about.

- Craig Gilborn

Historian Craig Gilborn, the former director of the Adirondack Museum in Blue Mountain Lake, New York, is a builder of outdoor furniture and author of *Adirondack Furniture and The Rustic Tradition,* published by Abrams. He lives in Long Lake, New York.

Natural Beauty of Wood

I was actively involved with repairing all manner of camp furnishings when an antique dealer friend convinced me to make my first chair. After taking the plunge, I spent three years researching before I attempted my first piece. That was many years ago, and I still have it: a split post-and-rung model.

Now I build mostly "twig" furniture, the kind with the bark still on. The various indigenous woods I work with provide me with color, form, and texture, allowing an artistic freedom of expression virtually unlimited by straight lines. Originally this work evolved to complement my lifestyle, and it has since become a very rewarding sideline, providing a business and personal recognition far beyond anything I ever dreamed of.

Working with wood in its natural state is particularly challenging. Much preparation and thought goes into every piece I build. A thorough knowledge of the wood I intend to work with is a must. As an example, if I want to have natural bark on a project, then I am restricted to harvesting my materials during a few months in the cold season. Also, tools to work wood in its natural state are not readily available. More often than not, figuring out how to do something takes longer than actually doing it. One of my biggest problems is storage: A stash of natural stock for chairs takes up far more space than milled limber.

There is always some detail that challenges my abilities and ingenuity to execute it, whether I am working with one of my own designs or something I've received from some architectural firm. Often when I am in the forest during my daily activities, I find my eye captured by a special curve some sapling has grown into and a piece of furniture will take form, piece by piece, in my mind. I can often see the finished product before I even harvest the unique form that caught my eye. Then, it may be three weeks, sometimes as much as five years, before the materials are dry enough to work with. I may consider subsequent designs, but I often go back to the original one I saw. The actual hands-on work required to make the piece may take a few hours or weeks, but when it's finished, it always leaves me with a sense of fulfillment and accomplishment, temporarily drained of the artist's creative spark and overwhelmed by the natural beauty of wood itself and the warmth it provides.

- Thomas Phillips

Thomas Phillips is a woods manager in Tupper Lake, New York where he restores outdoor and rustic furniture.

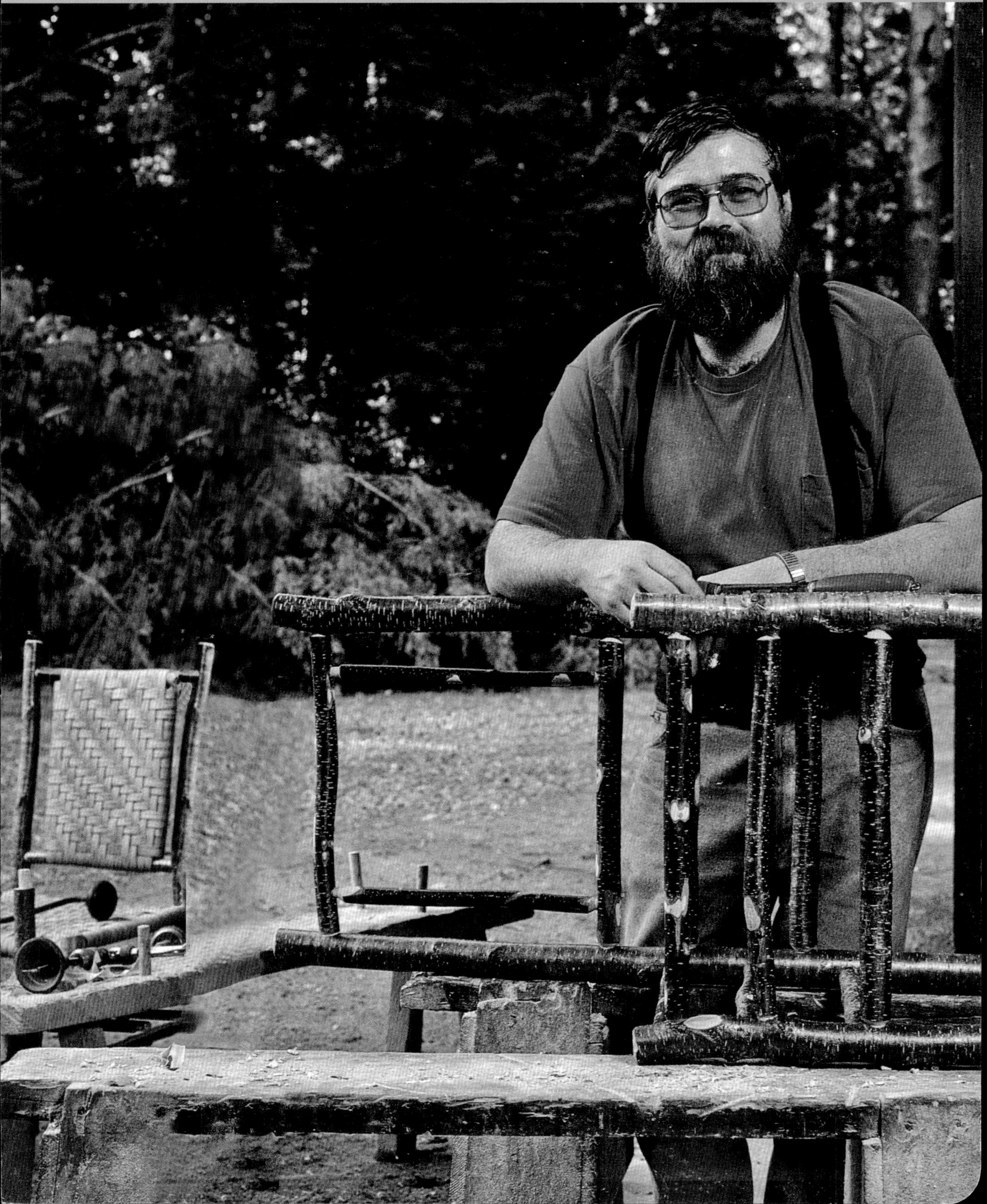

FACING THE ELEMENTS

While makers of indoor furniture need to consider the swelling and contraction of wood due to seasonal changes in relative humidity, outdoor furniture builders must also allow for the fact that their pieces will occasionally be drenched in water, dried by the wind, and baked by the sun. With appropriate materials, design, joinery, and hardware, you can fashion pieces that will be as durable and longlasting as any indoor piece.

Choose a project by reviewing some of the styles and types of outdoor pieces that have been popular with woodworkers. Then, select a wood species that is naturally decay-resistant. The chart on page 18 rates various woods in terms of their capacity to weather the outdoors. Refer to page 19 for information on calculating how much stock you will need.

Keep in mind that some of the same substances in decay-resistant woods that ward off rot can also give rise to allergic reations in builders and users. Redwood, for example, can cause respiratory ailments, while teak can produce skin and eye allergies. Western red cedar can trigger all three types of reaction.

The basic rule in choosing a joint is to avoid one that will trap water and eventually rot the wood when the weather is warm, or split the joint apart when it freezes in cold weather. Many outdoor pieces rely on joints like the half-lap that, when reinforced by screws and glue, are sufficiently durable while allowing water to drain away. Any hardware you use should be stainless steel to avoid rust. You should also use waterproof adhesives, such as epoxy or resorcinol.

Once your outdoor piece is ready for the yard or garden, the last step is to coat it with a weather-resistant finish. Pages 22 and 23 present information on the variety of finishes suitable for the outdoors, from glossy polyurethanes to a natural, unvarnished finish.

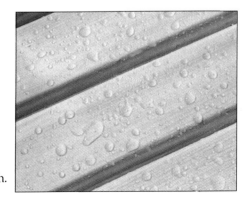

A coating of spar varnish is brushed onto a back slat of the backyard bench shown at left. To help you apply an even coat that will shield the piece from the elements, use a good-quality brush.

Two coats of waterproof polyurethane provide an extra measure of protection for an Adirondack chair made from Northern white cedar, a decay-resistant wood.

Vertical left margin: **FACING THE ELEMENTS**

Selecting Wood

Few decisions are as important to building outdoor furniture as the choice of wood. The chart below rates several species in terms of resistance to decay, strength, capacity to withstand shock, working properties (like planing and sanding or drilling, gluing, and fastening), and relative cost. There is no one ideal choice. Although a wood like teak combines strength with excellent decay resistance, it is very expensive, and difficult to find and work. Pine, however, is readily available and economical, and is easy to work, but most species are highly susceptible to decay and relatively weak. Many woodworkers consider native species with superior strength and decay resistance, such as cedar and white oak, to be a good compromise.

Keep in mind that the same qualities that make a wood like teak tough on blades and cutters will yield sturdy furniture.

Wood For Outdoors

Wood Species	Decay Resistance	Strength	Shock Resistance	Working Properties
Ash, white	Poor	Fair	Excellent	Average
Beech, American	Fair	Fair	Fair	Good
Birch, yellow	Fair	Good	Excellent	Good
Butternut	Poor	Fair	Fair	Good
Cedar, aromatic	Excellent	Fair	Fair	Average
Cedar, Western red	Excellent	Poor	Poor	Good
Cherry, American	Good	Fair	Fair	Good
Elm, American	Good	Fair	Fair	Fair
Douglas-fir	Fair	Fair	Fair	Average
Maple, hard	Poor	Excellent	Excellent	Good
Oak, red	Fair	Good	Fair	Average
Oak, white	Excellent	Excellent	Good	Average
Pine, Eastern white	Fair	Fair	Fair	Good
Pine, Southern yellow	Fair	Fair	Good	Average
Poplar, yellow	Fair	Fair	Fair	Good
Redwood	Excellent	Poor	Poor	Good
Teak	Excellent	Excellent	Excellent	Fair
Walnut, black	Good	Fair	Excellent	Good

Whichever species you select, take the time to choose your boards carefully. Avoid lumber that is cupped, bowed, or warped in any way. For maximum stability, choose air-dried lumber with a maximum of 20 percent moisture content. The wood should contain as little sapwood as possible because the sap will attract wood-eating bugs.

Calculating Board Feet

Ordering lumber by the board foot
The "board foot" is a unit of measurement used to calculate the volume of a given amount of stock. The standard board foot is equivalent to a piece that is 1 inch thick, 12 inches wide, and 12 inches long. To calculate the number of board feet in a piece of wood, multiply its three dimensions together. Then, divide the result by 144 if all the dimensions are in inches, or by 12 if just one dimension is in feet.

The formula for a standard board:

$$1" \times 12" \times 12" \div 144 = 1 \text{ (or } 1" \times 12" \times 1' \div 12 = 1)$$

So, if you had a 6-foot-long plank that is 1 inch thick and 4 inches wide, you would calculate the board feet as follows: $1" \times 4" \times 6' \div 12 = 2$ (or 2 board feet). Other examples are shown in the illustration. Remember that board feet are calculated on the basis of the nominal rather than actual dimensions of the stock; consequently, the board feet contained in a 2-by-4 that actually measures 1½-by-3½ inches would be calculated using the larger dimensions.

Nominal and Actual Softwood Lumber Sizes

Nominal (inches)	Actual (inches) Surfaced Dry
1-by-2	¾-by-1½
1-by-3	¾-by-2½
1-by-4	¾-by-3½
1-by-6	¾-by-5½
1-by-8	¾-by-7¼
1-by-10	¾-by-9¼
2-by-2	1½-by-1½
2-by-4	1½-by-3½
2-by-6	1½-by-5½
2-by-8	1½-by-7¼
2-by-10	1½-by-9¼
3-by-4	2½-by-3½
4-by-4	3½-by-3½

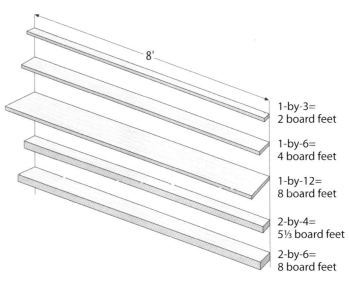

8'

1-by-3=
2 board feet

1-by-6=
4 board feet

1-by-12=
8 board feet

2-by-4=
5⅓ board feet

2-by-6=
8 board feet

Joinery and Hardware

Joinery presents unique challenges to the outdoor furniture maker. Many of the standard joints used for indoor furniture are incapable of withstanding the abuses wrought by weather. Water can become trapped in mortises, causing joints to swell and leading to wood decay. The through mortise-and-tenon *(page 21)*, solves that problem by allowing water to drain out. Cutting angled shoulders helps prevent water from becoming trapped. Lap joints and rabbet joints also work well. For extra protection against water, you can coat the mating surfaces of joints with a preservative such as pine tar or an adhesive caulking compound.

Outdoor furniture makes frequent use of fasteners to connect components. Make sure you choose ones that are either made from—or coated with—a metal that will not rust. Iron fasteners will eventually weaken or break and stain the wood.

Glues play an important part in most joinery, and here again, weather affects your choices. Standard yellow carpenter's glue is not waterproof and will eventually fail when exposed to the elements; look

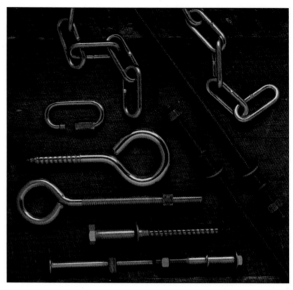

Choosing the right hardware is an important part of building outdoor furniture that will last. Chain and eye-hooks suspend hanging furniture, such as porch swings. Lag bolts, threaded rods and cross dowels join projects together. Make sure you select corrosion-resistant hardware, such as galvanized, stainless steel, or bronze.

for weather-resistant formulations. Or, select a specialized glue designed for outdoor use, such as resorcinol and epoxy-base adhesives. The former is somewhat easier to use, but epoxy has useful gap-filling properties.

Glue	Durability	Working Properties	Cost
Epoxy	Weatherproof; creates extremely strong bond	Requires mixing before use; sets quickly, requiring quick assembly	Expensive
Resorcinol	Weatherproof; extremely strong	Dries to a reddish colour; requires long clamping time	Expensive
Weatherproof yellow glue	Weatherproof; strong	Do not use standard, non-waterproof version of this glue	Inexpensive
Cross-linking PVA glue (Titebond II)	Weatherproof; forms extremely strong bond	One-part adhesive; good gap-filling ability; relatively quick drying time	Inexpensive
Plastic resin	Water-resistant; strong	Requires long clamping time; requires a topcoat for protection	Inexpensive
Urethane glue	Water-resistant; strong	Sticks to most other materials	Moderately expensive

Common Outdoor Furniture Joints

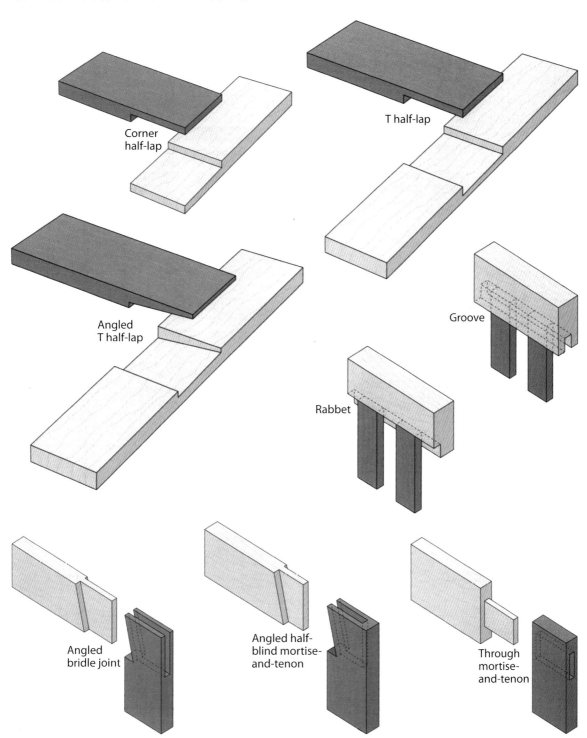

Corner half-lap

T half-lap

Angled T half-lap

Groove

Rabbet

Angled bridle joint

Angled half-blind mortise-and-tenon

Through mortise-and-tenon

Finishing

If you have built your furniture from rot-resistant and stable wood, you may choose to leave the wood unfinished. This cuts down on maintenance, because once a finish is applied, it must be renewed periodically. Still, some woods with little figure may look better covered with paint or a stain. A pigmented topcoat will also conceal any mismatched grain.

The most common finishing choices are penetrating oils, varnishes, and paint. Other finishes, especially paints, need a sealer first, followed by primer, then the finishing coats.

Water is not the only threat to outdoor furniture. Sunlight can damage wood by destroying the lignin in the wood, which fortifies the cell walls. To shield the wood completely from the sun, use paint. Generally, the higher the gloss, the better the protection, since the gloss will serve to reflect the sun's rays. Some finishes, such as spar varnish, contain ultraviolet (UV) filters, which help shield the furniture from the sun's harmful radiation. For maximum UV protection, apply four or five coats.

One of the solutions to finishing is not to do it. This arbor is made from cedar, which contains natural pesticides, making it extremely resistant to rot. The only maintenance required is to scrub away dirt and mildew occasionally. The wood will eventually turn a silvery-gray color. In general, dark woods tend to lighten over time, while light woods darken.

Outdoor Finishes

Type	Durability	Drying Time	Surface Sheen	Cost
Paint	Durable	Varies: Latex, 1–2 hours; alkyd, 3–4 hours. Recoat after 24 hours	Flat to gloss with range of opaque colours	Inexpensive
Spar varnish	Durable	4 to 6 hours, cures overnight	Satin to gloss; clear	Moderately expensive
Opaque stain	Resists fading, but does not protect wood from abrasion	4 to 6 hours	Flat to semi-gloss, many opaque colours	Moderately expensive
Polyurethane	Very durable; especially resistant to fungus	24 hours	Flat to gloss; clear, but yellows with age	Expensive

Steps for Applying Varnish or Paint

Varnish

- Sand with 120-grit sandpaper, then clean the surface with a tack cloth.

- Mix varnish by stirring only. Shaking varnish creates bubbles that may mar the finish.

- Avoid inexpensive varnish brushes. Instead, buy ones made from china bristle or badger hair. Or, use disposable foam brushes.

- Do not work in direct sunlight or in cool, damp locations.

- Apply at least four coats, preferably five.

- Sand between coats with a sanding block and 280-grit sandpaper, cleaning the surface afterwards with a tack cloth.

Paint

- Fill countersunk screw holes with wooden plugs.

- Sand with 120-grit sandpaper. Then raise the grain with a damp rag, and sand once more to remove the erect fibers.

- Fill small imperfections with wood dough or glazing compound.

- Wipe the surfaces with a tack cloth.

- Stir—do not shake—the paint.

- Paint knots first with shellac to seal them, then apply three coats of primer, sanding between each coat.

- Sand the final coat with 400-grit sandpaper, then finish with gloss paint.

Shop Tip

Straining varnish and paint
Varnish and paint often contain impurities that must be removed before use. For best results, strain them. Simply pour the finish through a large coffee filter into a clean container.

Outdoor furniture must be designed to rough it, and the Adirondack chair, chaise lounge, and curved chair featured in this chapter are all up to the task. In many parts of the country with harsh winters, the emergence of outdoor chairs marks the return of pleasant weather. They are carted out of the garage or basement on the first sunny day of spring and then left exposed to the elements. Such treatment places a particular set of demands on the joinery. Even with a durable and decay-resistant species, there is the danger that the wood will eventually rot.

All three chairs in this chapter solve this problem by using half-lap joints. What it lacks in stoutness, the half-lap makes up for in versatility. It will not trap water and, when reinforced with a weatherproof epoxy and screws, it is exceptionally strong. The joint is also simple to produce. You can make both parts of the connection on the table saw *(page 39)*.

If you need to cut a series of half-laps, it will probably be worth your time to make a shop-built jig and do the job with a router *(page 85)*.

The chaise longue *(page 46)* relies heavily on the half-lap. The joint is used to fasten all the back slats to the rails. The back of this classic poolside relaxer can assume six different positions, from the horizontal to nearly vertical.

The Adirondack chair *(page 26)* is among the most familiar pieces of outdoor furniture. The curved chair *(page 36)* is an original design, ideally suited for a hidden corner of the garden. The version shown in this chapter is made of eight units; you can build a wider chair, or even a bench, by incorporating more units in the design.

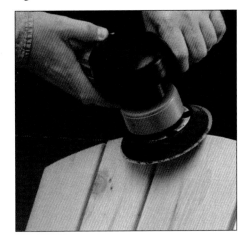

After evening out any slight irregularities in the ends of an Adirondack chair with a belt sander, you can use a random-orbit sander for final smoothing.

The chaise longue shown at left is perfectly suited for stretching out and relaxing. Like the other chairs featured in this chapter, it is made from lightweight but durable Northern white cedar. With its sturdy wheels and portable design, the longue is easy to move to just the right location. A thin mattress will provide an extra measure of comfort.

Adirondack Chair

There are few pieces of outdoor furniture more inviting than an Adirondack chair. Its reclining seat and tilted backrest beckon the user to sink into the seat and lean back, elbows propped on the wide armrests, which provide plenty of room for books and a cold drink.

Most of the parts of the chair are irregularly shaped. To reproduce the classic design illustrated below, refer to the cutting patterns shown opposite. Remember that the dimensions cited in the cutting list represent the stock size before shaping on the band saw. Size the parts first, then transfer the patterns to the stock.

Assembled with stainless steel screws and waterproof glue, and finished with a weatherproof varnish, the Adirondack chair shown above is ready to face the elements.

Anatomy of an Adirondack Chair

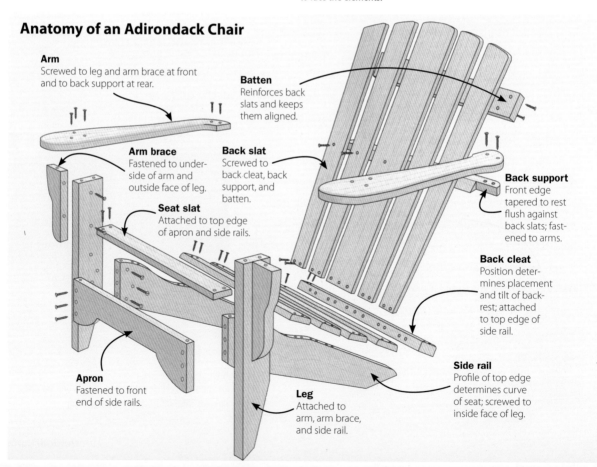

Arm
Screwed to leg and arm brace at front and to back support at rear.

Batten
Reinforces back slats and keeps them aligned.

Arm brace
Fastened to underside of arm and outside face of leg.

Back slat
Screwed to back cleat, back support, and batten.

Back support
Front edge tapered to rest flush against back slats; fastened to arms.

Seat slat
Attached to top edge of apron and side rails.

Back cleat
Position determines placement and tilt of backrest; attached to top edge of side rail.

Apron
Fastened to front end of side rails.

Leg
Attached to arm, arm brace, and side rail.

Side rail
Profile of top edge determines curve of seat; screwed to inside face of leg.

Cutting Pattern for Curved Parts of Chair

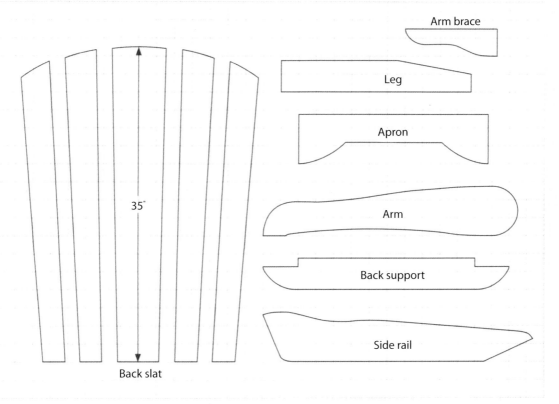

Arm brace

Leg

Apron

Arm

Back support

Side rail

35"

Back slat

1 square = 2 inches. Enlarge grid to produce a cutting pattern of the appropriate size for your project.

Cutting List	Qty	Th	W	L
Arm	2	¾"	5½"	29"
Arm brace	2	1¼"	3"	10½"
Leg	2	1¼"	3½"	21½"
Side rail	2	1¼"	5½"	30¾"
Apron	1	¾"	5½"	21½"
Back cleat	1	1¼"	3½"	21½"
Center back slat	1	¾"	5½"	35"
Side back slats	4	¾"	3½"	35"
Back support	1	1¼"	3½"	28"
Batten	1	¾"	3¼"	19½"
Seat slats	5	¾"	3¼"	21½"

Building an Adirondack Chair

A table-mounted router equipped with a round-over bit softens the edges of one of the arms of an Adirondack chair. The setup shown at left includes a shop-made fence and bit guard to provide a bearing surface for the stock while protecting the operator's fingers from the spinning bit. For best results, make two passes to reach your final depth. In addition to the arms, the edges of the back and seat slats and the back cleat are also rounded over.

Preparing the Stock

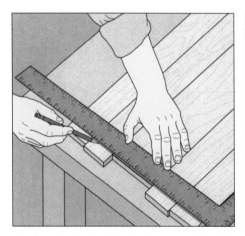

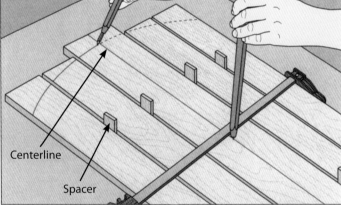

Centerline

Spacer

Curving the back slats. Cut the pieces of the chair to size, referring to the anatomy illustration *(page 26)* and cutting patterns *(page 27)*. For the back slats, start by tapering them so the middle one is 4⅝ inches wide at the bottom and 5½ inches at the top; the outside slats should be 2½ inches at the bottom and 3½ inches at the top. You can make the cuts on a table saw using a commercial jig or the shop-built version shown opposite. Next, set the slats edge to edge on a work surface; the ends will be uneven. To even out the bottom edge, use a pencil and a carpenter's square to mark a line across the outside slats that aligns with the end of the middle piece *(above, left)*. Trim the outside slats along the marks, then draw a line down the center of the middle slat. Reposition the slats and clamp them together with their bottom ends aligned and ¼-inch-thick spacers between the pieces. Adjust a compass to a 16-inch radius, set the point on the middle slat centerline 18¾ inches from the bottom end, and draw the curve at the top end of the slats *(above, right)*. Cut the slats on your band saw, then round over their edges *(photo, top)*.

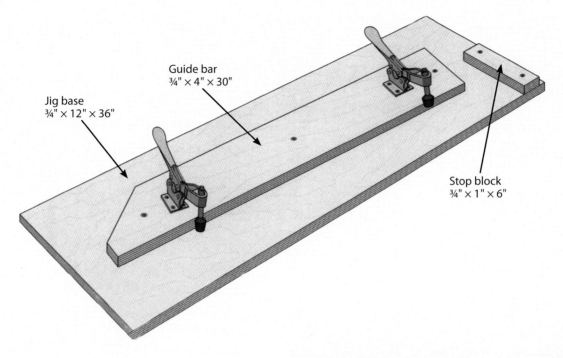

Guide bar
¾" × 4" × 30"

Jig base
¾" × 12" × 36"

Stop block
¾" × 1" × 6"

Taper Jig

To taper the back slats and legs of your chair on the table saw, build the jig shown above from ¾-inch plywood. To assemble the jig, set the saw blade to its maximum height, butt one side of the jig base against the blade and position the rip fence flush against the other side of the base. Lower the blade. Mark a cutting line for the taper on the workpiece, then set it on the base, aligning the line with the edge of the base nearest the blade. Holding the workpiece securely, position the guide bar against the edge and the stop block snugly against the end. Screw the guide bar and stop block to the base and press the toggle clamps down to secure the workpiece to the jig; protect the stock with wood pads. To make the cut, set the blade height and slide the jig and workpiece across the table, making sure that neither hand is in line with the blade *(right)*. **(Caution: Blade guard removed for clarity.)**

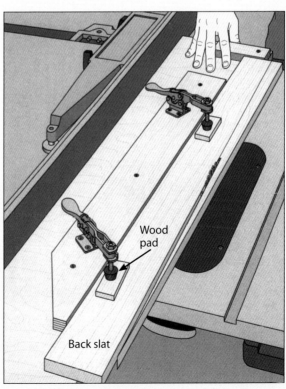

Wood pad

Back slat

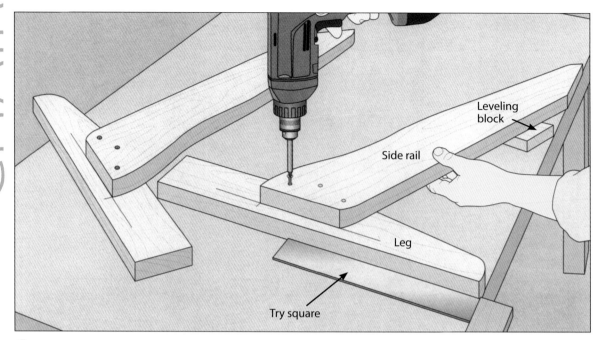

Leveling block

Side rail

Leg

Try square

1 Attaching the side rails to the legs. To position the side rails on the legs, mark a pair of intersecting guidelines on the legs' inside faces. Mark one line parallel to the front edge and 1 inch from it to allow for the apron and a ¼-inch reveal; the second line should be parallel to the top end and 6¾ inches below it. To ensure the leg and rail will be level on the ground, align the bottom ends of the pieces with an edge of your work surface; use a try square to make sure the front edge of the leg is perpendicular to the edge of the table. Drill three clearance holes for screws through each rail and spread waterproof glue on the contacting surfaces between the leg and rail. With the leg inside-face up on a work surface, fasten the rail to the leg, aligning the front end and top edge of the rail with the guidelines on the leg *(above)*.

2 Installing the apron. Bore three clearance holes through the apron about ⅝ inch from each end. Apply waterproof glue to the ends of the rails, set the legs upright on a work surface and position the apron between the legs and flush against the rails. The top edges of the apron and rails should be level. Using a bar clamp to hold the piece square to the legs, screw the apron to the rails *(right)*; protect the stock with wood pads.

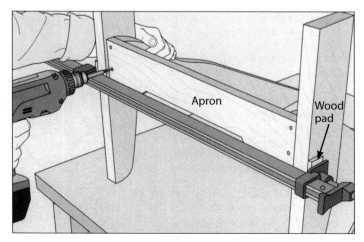

Apron

Wood pad

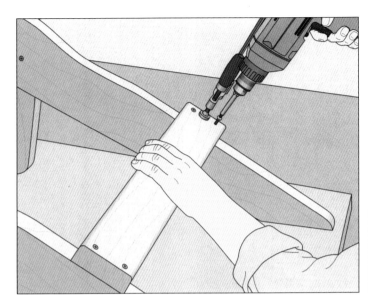

3 Attaching the back cleat to the side rails.

Remember to round over the top edges of the cleat before installing the piece. Then mark a guideline for the cleat across the top edge of each rail 11½ inches from the back end. Drill two clearance holes through the cleat near each end, spread glue, and use a clamp to hold the cleat in position against the rails. Making sure the ends of the cleat are flush with the outside edges of the rails, fasten the piece in place *(left)*.

Shop Tip

Using a dowel to anchor a screw driven into end grain
Many of the joints used to assemble the Adirondack chair, such as those between the apron and side rails or the arms and legs, require you to fasten into end grain. Screws do not hold well in end grain, so a fastener on its own may not be strong enough to keep an end-to-face butt joint together. Glue can help somewhat, but to reinforce the connection adequately, bore a ⅜-inch-diameter hole vertically through the end grain piece about ½ inch from its end. Glue a dowel in the hole and let the adhesive dry. Then drive your screws through the mating piece into the dowel. The screws will anchor securely in the long grain of the dowel.

4 Screwing the arm brace to the legs.

Clamp each arm brace to its leg and side rail so it is aligned with the middle of the leg. The top ends of the brace and leg should be flush. Next, bore three clearance holes through the leg, stopping the drill when the bit contacts the brace. Install a smaller-diameter bit to continue drilling pilot holes into the brace, using the clearance holes as guides. Unclamp the brace, then spread glue on its flat edge, reclamp it in position, and fasten it to the leg *(above)*.

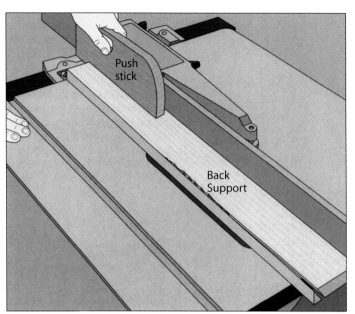

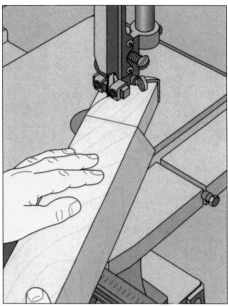

5 **Preparing the back support.** Bevel the front edge of the back support to provide an adequate bearing surface for the back slats and allow them to tilt at the correct angle. On your table saw, position the rip fence on the left-hand side of the saw blade for a width of cut of 2⅝ inches and angle the blade to 30°. (It is always safest to make a bevel cut with the blade angled away from the fence.) Feed the stock into the cutting edge with your left hand while pressing the board against the fence. Finish the pass with a push stick *(above, left)*. **(Caution: Blade guard removed for clarity.)** Next, outline the curves on the outside edge of the back support—one at each end—and mark a straight line across the board 3¾ inches from each end. Use your band saw to make a cut from each end of the support to the straight line; align the cuts with the start of the bevel. Finally, cut the curved ends of the board on the band saw *(above, right)*.

6 **Attaching the arms to the back support.** Remember to round over the arms *(photo, page 28)*, then drill two clearance holes through each one. Spread waterproof glue on the mating surfaces of the arms and support, position one of the arms on the support, and screw the pieces together, using a try square to make sure the pieces are perpendicular to each other *(right)*. Repeat to fix the other arm to the support.

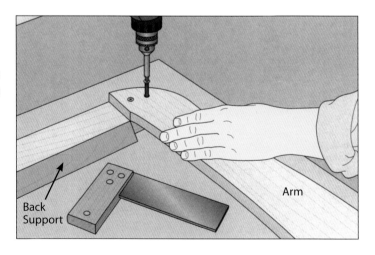

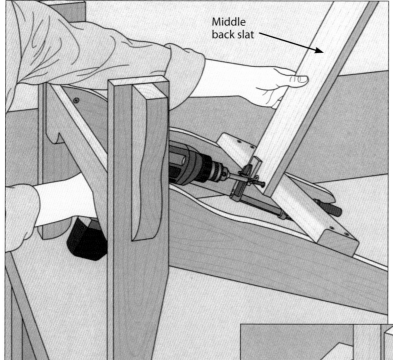

Middle back slat

7 Installing the middle back slat.
Before you can attach the arms and back support to the chair, the middle back slat must be fastened in place. Set the chair upright on a work surface and clamp the slat to the center of the back cleat, aligning the bottom end of the slat with the bottom face of the cleat; protect the stock with wood pads. Holding the slat flush against the cleat, use three screws to fasten it in place *(left)*. Do not use glue in case you need to adjust the slat later when you install the remaining back slats.

8 Fastening the arms and back support to the chair. Set the arms and back support upside down on a work surface, then position the leg assembly on the arms. Center the middle back slat on the back support and clamp the pieces together. At the front of the chair, use a tape measure to ensure that the inside edges of the arms extend beyond the legs by the same amount on both sides. Using the legs and arm supports as guides, make location marks on the undersides of the arms once you are satisfied with the position of the leg assembly *(right)*. Set the chair upright and drill three clearance holes through each arm and one through the middle back slat. Spread glue on the contacting surfaces of the arms, legs, and arm supports, then reposition the arms in place—using the location marks as guides—and screw the pieces together.

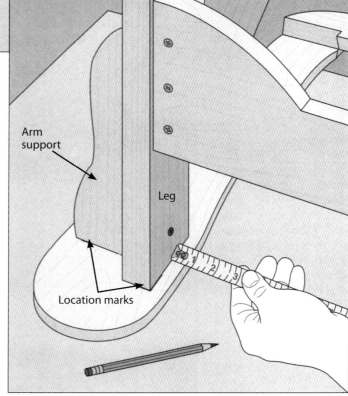

Arm support

Leg

Location marks

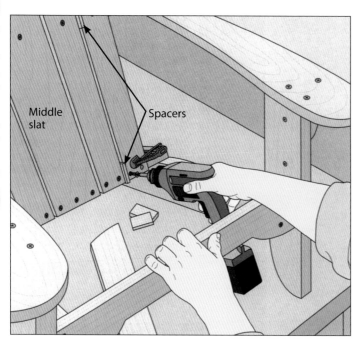

Middle slat

Spacers

9 **Fastening the back slats.** Spread glue on the contacting surfaces between the side back slats and the back support and cleat. Screw the slats in place *(left)*, slipping ¼-inch spacers between the pieces as on page 28 to position them properly. Use two screws to secure each slat to the cleat and a single fastener at the back support. Make sure the bottom of each end slat is flush with the bottom edge of the cleat. Once all the side slats are installed, unscrew the middle one, apply glue, and reattach it.

10 **Installing the batten.** To cut the batten to final length, clamp your stock against the back slats about 12 inches above the back support and mark the outside edge of the slats on the board. At the same time, mark clearance holes on the batten—two for each slat—alternating the holes between the top and bottom edge of the stock. Cut the batten to length on your band saw and drill the clearance holes. Then, spread some glue on the batten, clamp it to the back slats, and screw it in place *(right)*. Use a belt sander to create a smooth curve along the top of the back slats and sand the ends of the batten and the joint between the arms and the back support.

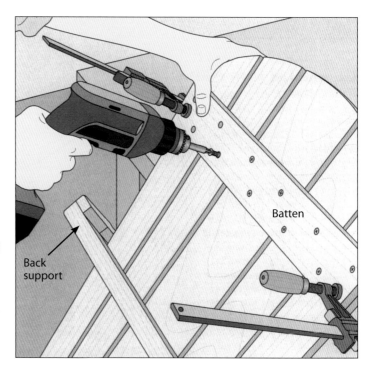

Batten

Back support

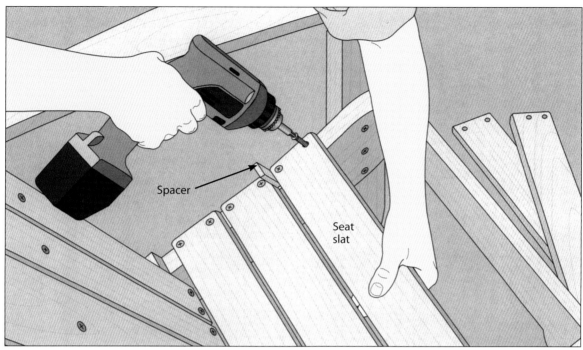

Shop Tip

Sealing knots with shellac

Because it is intended to be sturdy and rustic, outdoor furniture is often built with lower-grade wood. Although this is economical, many such boards have knots. Loose knots should be cut off, since they weaken the wood. Although tight knots have no effect on the strength of stock and can be left intact, they often ooze pitch, even after a finish is applied to the piece of furniture. This pitch will bleed through paint or varnish, staining the finish and producing a sticky mess. To avoid this problem, brush two thin coats of shellac over tight knots to seal them.

11 **Attaching the seat slats.** To complete the chair, round over the edges of the seat slats *(photo, page 28)*, then drill two clearance holes at each end of the pieces. Starting with the slat nearest the back, spread some glue on the slat's bottom face and screw it to the side rails; use ¼-inch spacers to maintain the proper gap betwen the slat and the back. Install the remaining slats the same way, separating the pieces with the spacers *(above)*. The last slat should extend beyond the apron by about 1 inch. Rip the slat to width and round its edges again, if necessary, before screwing it in place.

Curved Chair

The curved chair featured in this section is built by joining eight identical H-shaped units with steel rods. Each unit is separated from the adjoining one by three 2-inch-diameter spacers—two at the rear leg and one at the front. The curve is achieved by using 1½-inch-long spacers in back and ¾-inch-long spacers in front.

The modular design of the chair is very versatile. You can use spacers of uniform length to create a straight chair or build additional units to make a bench.

As shown opposite, each seating unit is joined to its rear and front legs with half-laps—a T half-lap at the back and a corner half-lap at the front—and all the joints are reinforced by screws. Once the joinery is done, the pieces are shaped and trimmed with a router and a template.

The curve of the chair shown above is made possible by using spacers at the back that are twice as long as those at the front. This chair was finished with two coats of primer and one coat of exterior-grade paint.

Anatomy of a Curved Chair

Spacer

Cap

Threaded rod

Rear leg

Seating unit

Front leg

Curved Chair Joinery

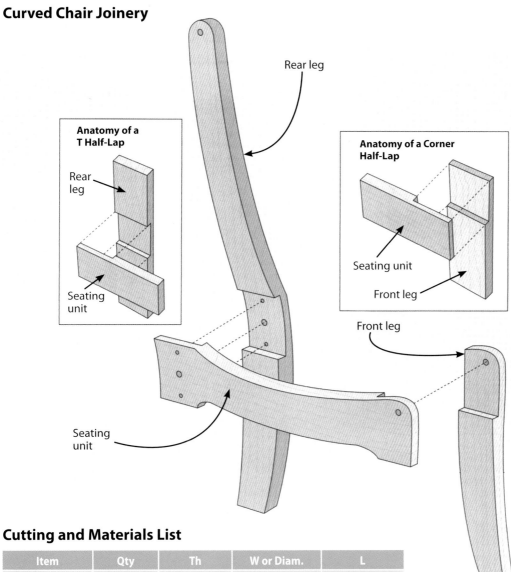

**Anatomy of a
T Half-Lap**

Rear
leg

Seating
unit

**Anatomy of a Corner
Half-Lap**

Seating unit

Front leg

Rear leg

Front leg

Seating
unit

Cutting and Materials List

Item	Qty	Th	W or Diam.	L
Rear leg	8	1¼"	5½"	36"
Front leg	8	1¼"	5½"	17¾"
Seating unit	8	1¼"	4⅞"	20½"
Long spacers	16	1½"	2"	
Short spacers	8	¾"	2"	
Caps	6		1"	
Rods	3		¼"	36"
Washers	6		¼"	
Nuts	6		¼"	

Fashioning a Curved Chair

One of the units of a curved chair is trimmed to within about ⅛ inch of the cutting line on the band saw. Once all the pieces are cut, they are pared to final shape with a router fitted with a flush-trimming bit, guided by a template.

Assembling the Units

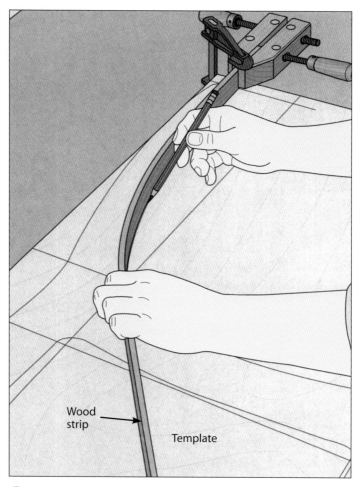

Wood strip

Template

1 **Making the template.** Mark out a template of the chair units on a piece of plywood or hardboard, referring to the anatomy illustration on page 36 for the profile and dimensions of the pieces. Start by drawing the legs and seating unit with straight lines, then use a thin strip of springy wood to help you outline the natural curves along the edges of the pieces. Using a handscrew and a bar clamp, secure the strip on edge on the template so that one face is flush with the top of one of your cutting lines. Then gently bend the strip toward the other end of the line. Keeping the strip firmly in place, run a pencil along it to define the curve *(above)*. Cut the template to shape on your band saw, then sand the edges smooth. Set the template aside for now; before using it to outline *(page 40)* and trim *(page 41)* the units, you need to cut the half-laps in your stock and assemble the pieces.

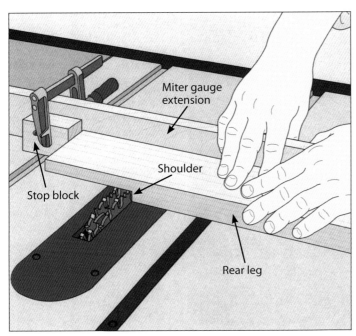

2 **Cutting the half-laps in the front legs and seating units.** Mark the shoulders of the half-laps on your blanks for the front legs and seating units, using the template as a guide. Then install a dado head on your table saw, adjust it to maximum width and set the cutting height at one-half the stock thickness. Attach an extension board to the miter gauge, align the shoulder line on the first leg with the blade and clamp a stop block to the extension against the end of the workpiece. Starting at the end of the board, feed it face down along with the miter gauge to saw away the waste. Make a series of passes to remove the remaining waste wood until you define the shoulder with the workpiece butted against the stop block and miter gauge extension *(left)*. Repeat with the remaining front legs, then cut half-laps at both ends of the seating units the same way, repositioning the stop block as necessary.

(Labels in illustration: Miter gauge extension, Shoulder, Stop block, Rear leg)

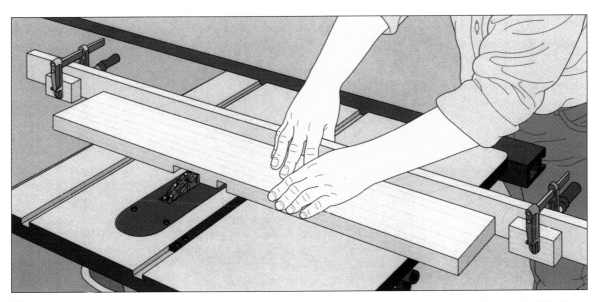

3 **Sawing the dadoes in the rear legs.** Outline the dadoes in the rear leg blanks to accommodate the half-laps in the seating units. The same setup used to cut the half-laps can be employed to saw the dadoes—except that you will need to clamp a second stop block to the miter gauge extension to set the overall width of the joint. Feeding the workpiece face down and butted against a stop block, start by cutting the two sides of the dado. Then make a series of passes to clear the waste in between *(above)*.

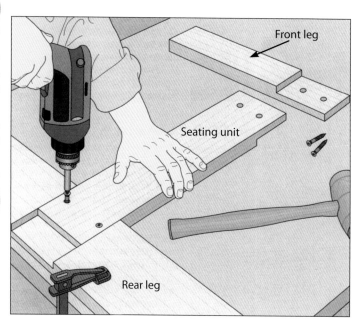

Front leg

Seating unit

Rear leg

4 **Assembling the units.** Test-fit the legs and seating units, and use a chisel to trim any ill-fitting joints. Then drill two clearance holes into the stock at each joint and spread waterproof glue on the half-laps of the seating units; make sure to locate the screws so they will not interfere with the placement of the threaded rod *(page 43)*. Clamp the rear leg face up to a work surface, position the seating unit on it, and screw the pieces together *(left)*. (Note that the back end of the seating unit is offset from the back edge of the leg; as shown below, about one-half the width of the legs will be cut away at the point where they meet the seat.) Finally, attach the front leg to the seating unit.

Trimming the Units to Size

1 **Outlining the chair profile on the units.** Once all the units are assembled, place one face up on a work surface, position the template on it, and use a pencil to trace its outline on the stock *(right)*. The back edge of the template should be almost flush with the back edge of the rear leg at its top end. Mark the remaining units, then cut them all to rough size on the band saw *(page 38)*, leaving about ⅛ inch of waste outside your cutting lines.

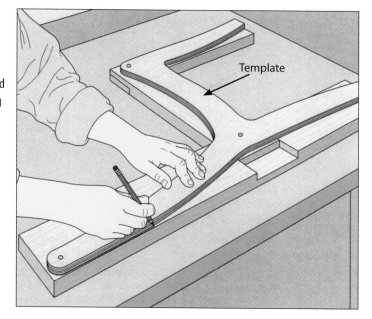

Template

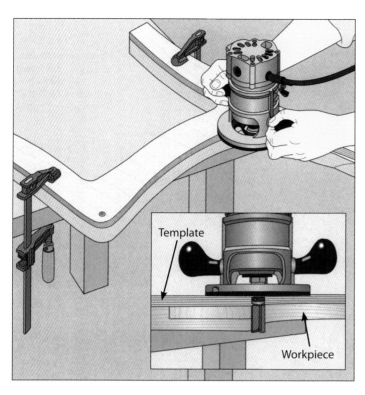

Template

Workpiece

2 **Shaping the chair units.** Finish shaping the units using a router fitted with a top-piloted flush-trimming bit. Set the unit on a work surface and center the template on top, then fasten the pieces together, driving a screw through each threaded rod hole in the template into the unit. Clamp the assembly to the table and adjust the router's depth of cut so the pilot bearing will rub only on the template *(inset)*. Guide the router against the direction of bit rotation along the edges of the unit, keeping the bearing in constant contact with the template *(left)*. Reposition the clamps as needed.

3 **Rounding over the end units.** To round over the outside edges of the two units that will be on the outside of the chair, install a bottom-piloted rounding-over bit in the router and set the depth of cut to reach your final depth in two passes. Secure the unit outside-face up to a work surface and make each pass by feeding the router along the edges of the piece, pressing the bit's pilot bearing against the stock throughout *(right)*. Again, reposition the clamps as necessary.

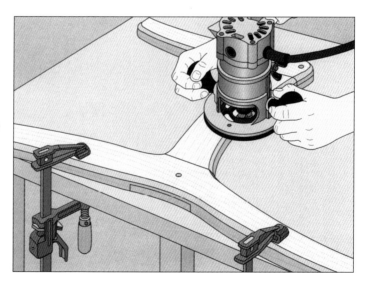

Assembling the Chair

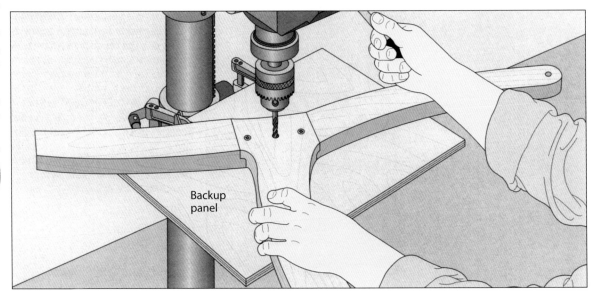

Backup panel

1 Preparing the units for the threaded rod.
Use the holes you used to secure the template *(page 40)* as guides to bore clearance holes for the threaded rod. Start by clamping a plywood backup panel to your drill press table and install a ¼-inch bit in the machine. Position the unit on the table so that one of the holes is aligned under the bit and hold the unit steady as you drill the hole *(above)*.

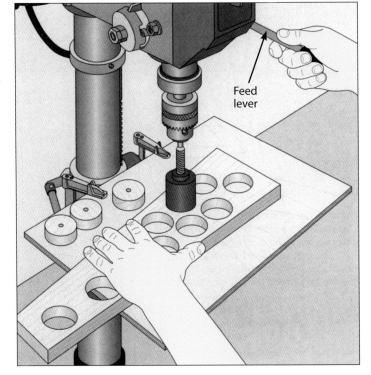

Feed lever

2 Making the spacers. Fit your drill press with a 1¾-inch-diameter hole saw to cut the spacers that separate the chair units. Make the spacers from two boards—¾ inch thick for the front spacers and 1½ inches thick for the rear ones. Hold the board on the machine table and cut through the stock, lowering the feed lever slowly *(right)*. At the same time, the hole saw's pilot bit will bore a hole through the center of each spacer for the threaded rod.

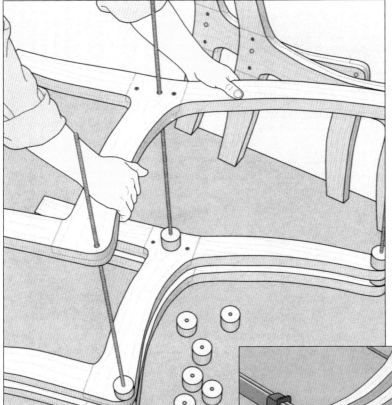

3 Stacking the units. Once you have cut enough spacers, you can begin assembling the chair. Start by feeding the three threaded rods through the holes in one end unit and anchoring each with a nut and washer. Set the unit inside-face up on the shop floor and slip a spacer onto each rod, using longer spacers at the back and shorter ones at the front. Next, fit a chair unit onto the rods and press it firmly on the spacers. Continue adding spacers and chair units *(left)* until the last unit is in place, then install a washer and nut onto the top end of each rod.

4 Tightening the rods. Close any gaps between the spacers and the chair units. Hand pressure should suffice at the back of the chair; use a wrench to tighten the nuts. At the front of the chair, install a bar clamp across the seat and tighten it as necessary to close any gaps; protect the stock with wood pads. Tighten the nuts at the front of the chair *(right)*, then give all the nuts a final tightening. Remove the bar clamps and use a hacksaw to cut the excess rod flush with the nuts. Cover the nuts with wood caps fashioned from short lengths of 1-inch dowel.

Wood pad

Installing Arms

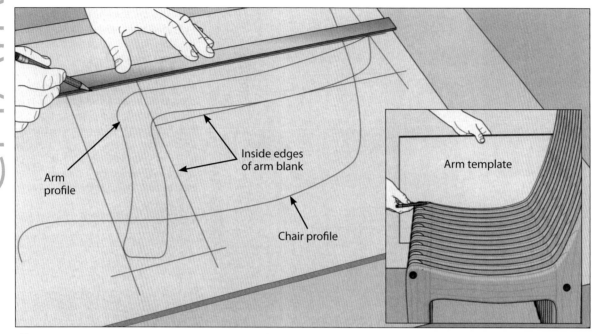

Arm profile

Inside edges of arm blank

Chair profile

Arm template

1 **Designing the arms.** You can add arms to the curved chair, applying the same design and joinery methods used to make the individual units. Start by preparing a template, holding a piece of hardboard against one side of the chair and marking its outline with a pencil *(inset)*. Then design the arm so it will be both comfortable and visually pleasing; the armrest part should be 8 to 9 inches above the seat. Next, use a pencil and straightedge to outline the L-shaped arm blank on the template *(above)*, making it as wide as necessary to contain the arm profile. Cut the template on a band saw *(photo, page 38)* and sand the edges smooth.

2 **Outlining the arm profile on the blanks.** Make each arm blank from two boards joined into an L shape by half-laps *(page 39)*; refer to your template when sizing the boards. Set one of the blanks on a work surface, position the template on it and use a pencil to trace its outline on the stock *(right)*. Mark the other blank, then cut the arms to size on a band saw *(page 38)*. Smooth the cut edges, sanding the stock to your cutting lines.

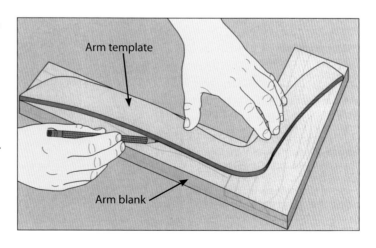

Arm template

Arm blank

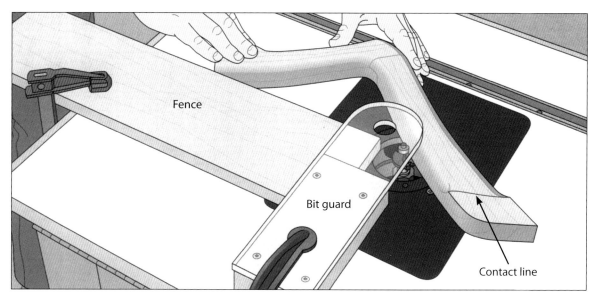

Fence

Bit guard

Contact line

3 **Rounding over the edges of the arms.** Round over the edges of the arms, except where they contact the chair. To mark out these areas, position each arm against the chair and draw a pencil across it along the top of the seat and the front edge of the rear leg. Remember to mark out right- and left-hand versions of the arm. Install a piloted round-over bit in a router and mount the tool in a table. To provide a bearing surface for the arms, fashion a guard for the bit and a fence for the stock to ride against the infeed side of the table. Screw the guard and fence together and clamp them to the table. Press the workpiece against the pilot bearing as you feed each arm across the table, then turn over the stock and shape the other edge *(above)*. When rounding over the inside faces of the arms, start and stop the cuts at the marked contact lines.

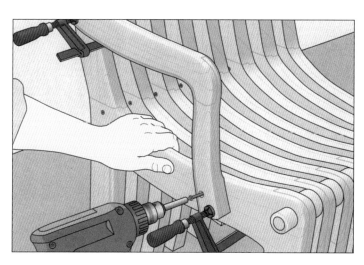

4 **Attaching the arms to the chair.** Drill two clearance holes through each arm—one at either end—and apply glue to the flat areas that will contact the chair. Clamp the arm in position on the chair and fasten it in place *(left)*.

Lounge Chair

No deck or patio is complete without at least one long lounge chair or "chaise longue." Building a couple like the one shown at right and in the color photograph on page 24 involves the better part of a weekend's work, but the finished products will provide years of comfortable loafing and sun worshipping.

The chair is made with almost two dozen slats. Those for the main body are simply screwed to a cleat fastened to the side rails; the backrest slats are joined to rails with half-laps. Butt hinges secure the backrest to the body. The backrest can be adjusted from the horizontal position to nearly vertical, and the notched rack supporting the backrest allows it to be set at several positions in between.

The lounge chair is lightweight and easy to move on wheels attached to the rear legs. The wheels are held in place with axle caps. Although this hardware is not as strong as cotter pins, it is easier to install and more than sturdy enough for the light-duty needs of the chair. Use a galvanized steel or aluminum rod for the axle.

As the slats are thin, try to select knot-free wood for these pieces.

Cutting and Materials List

Piece	Qty	Th	W or Diam.	L
Side rails	2	1¼"	4½"	90"
Slats	13	¾"	3"	21½"
Handle	1	x	1"	22½"
Backrest rail	2	¾"	3"	29½"
Backrest slats	8	¾"	3"	21½"
Cleats	2	1¼"	1¼"	78"
Spacer	2	1¼"	1¼"	24"
Rack	2	1¼"	1¼"	17¼"
Backrest support rails	2	¾"	1½"	18½"
Backrest support stiles	2	¾"	1½"	20"
Backrest support stop	2	1¼"	1¼"	2½"
Front legs	2	1⅜"	3½"	9"
Rear legs	2	1⅜"	3½"	7¼"
Axle	1	x	½"	36"
Wheels	2	x	8"	x
Washers	4 (min)	x	½"	x
Axle cap	2	x	½"	x

Anatomy of a Lounge Chair

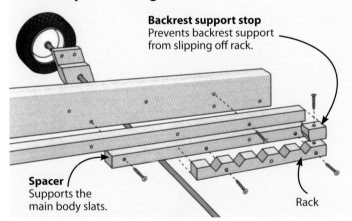

Backrest support stop
Prevents backrest support from slipping off rack.

Spacer
Supports the main body slats.

Rack

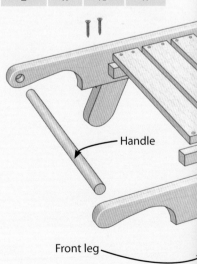

Handle

Front leg

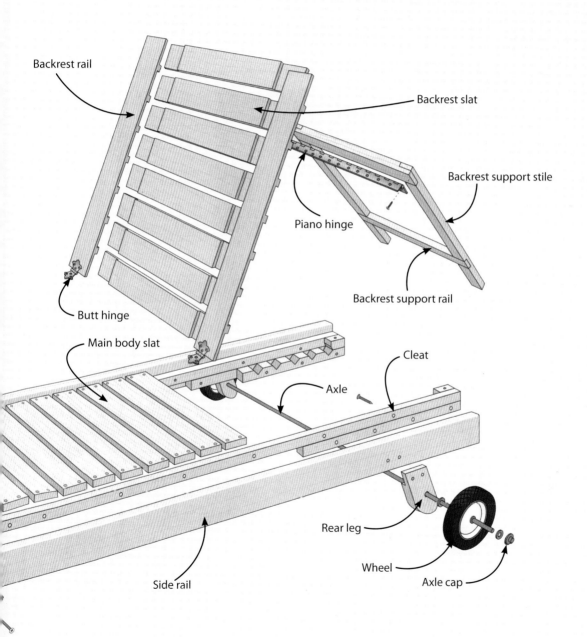

Backrest rail

Backrest slat

Backrest support stile

Piano hinge

Backrest support rail

Butt hinge

Main body slat

Cleat

Axle

Rear leg

Side rail

Wheel

Axle cap

Making a Lounge Chair

A saber saw cuts the curved profile at the front end of one of the side rails of a lounge chair. Once the rails are sized properly, the curve can be marked on the stock with reference to the anatomy illustration on page 47. Because the rails are almost 8 feet long, it is easier to make the cuts with a portable saw than to attempt to maneuver the boards on a band saw *(left)*. After sawing the curves, smooth the cut edges using a spindle sander or sanding block. All the edges of the rails are then rounded over.

Fashioning the Side Rails

1 Rounding over the side rails. Cut each of the side rails to size, clamp the stock face up to a work surface, and saw the curves at the front end *(photo, above)*. Then install a piloted rounding-over bit in a router and make each pass by feeding the router along the edges of the rail, pressing the bit's pilot bearing against the stock throughout the cut *(right)*. Reposition the clamps as necessary. Turn the rail over and repeat on the other side.

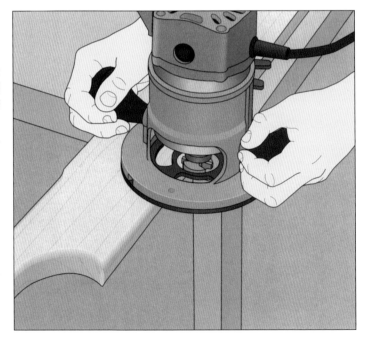

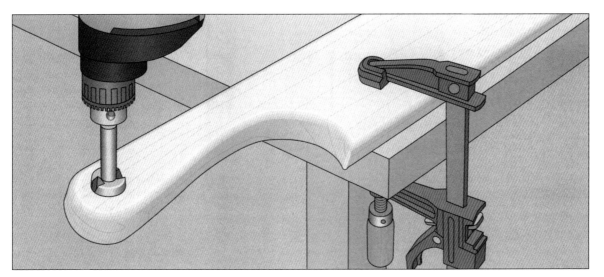

2 Drilling the handle holes. The handle at the front end of the chair is made from a length of 1-inch-diameter dowel. Bore the dowel holes in the side rails with an electric drill fitted with a 1-inch Forstner bit. Clamp the stock inside-face up on a work surface and mark out the holes, centering them between the edges about 1½ inches from the front end of the rail. Make sure the marks are in the same location on both rails. Holding the drill vertical, bore the hole *(above)*, stopping when the body of the bit is completely recessed in the wood; this will yield a ½-inch-deep hole.

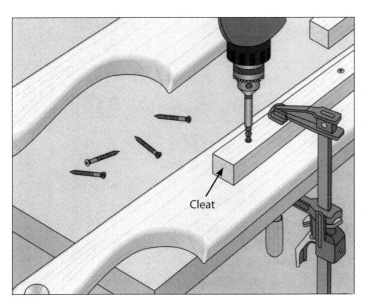

Cleat

3 Attaching the cleats to the rails. To position the cleats on the rails, mark a line along each rail's inside face 1½ inches from the bottom edge. Starting 2 inches from one end of the cleat, drill a clearance hole every 8 inches along its length. Then apply waterproof glue on the inside face of the cleat and position the stock on the side rail, aligning the back ends of the pieces. Anchor the cleat in place, holding the strip so its bottom edge is flush with the marked line on the rail as you drive each screw *(left)*. Work from the back of the cleat to the front.

Assembling the Body

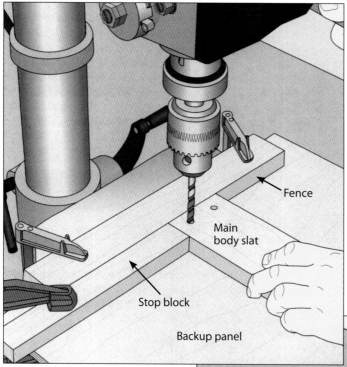

Fence

Main body slat

Stop block

Backup panel

1 Preparing the slats. Cut the slats for the body of the chair to size, then drill two holes at each end of every piece. To keep the location of the holes uniform, do the job on your drill press aided by the simple jig shown at left. Start by securing a backup panel to the machine table and drilling the first of the holes—which are all ¾ inch from the end of the slats and ⅝ inch from the nearest edge. For the jig, leave the slat in position and clamp two boards to the table as a fence and stop block. The fence should be flush against the end of the slat and the stop block should be butted against both the fence and the edge of the slat. Drill the second hole by turning the slat over and seating it in the jig. Repeat the process at the slat's other end and at both ends of the remaining slats.

2 Installing the slats. Once all the slats are ready, set the side rails on edge on a work surface. Spread glue on the first slat and, starting at the front of the chair, set it on the cleats. The slat's front edge should be flush with the end of the cleats; its end should butt against the rails. Check with a try square to make sure the slat is perpendicular to the rails, then screw the slat in place. To install the remaining slats, use a board the same thickness as the slats as a spacer (right). Check the assembly for square every four or five slats.

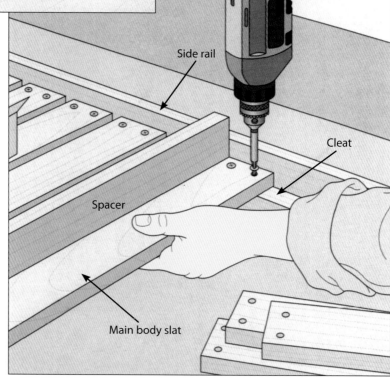

Side rail

Cleat

Spacer

Main body slat

Building the Backrest

1 Preparing the backrest rails and slats. The backrest slats are joined to the rails with half-laps. Outline the rabbets at the ends of the rails and the dadoes in between, making them as long as the rail width and as deep as one-half the stock thickness; leave ¾ inch of space between the outlines. Install a dado head on your table saw, adjust it to maximum width, and set the cutting height. Attach an extension to your miter gauge. Saw the rabbets first, then work from one end of the board to the other to cut the dadoes *(right)*. For each channel, start by defining one shoulder, then make a series of passes until you reach the other shoulder. Hold the rail flush against the miter gauge extension throughout **(Note: Guard removed for clarity.)** Follow the same procedure to saw matching rabbets at both ends of the slats.

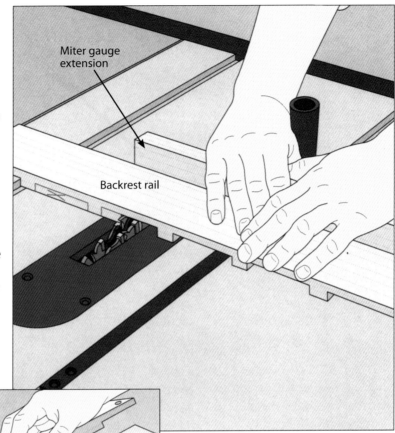

Miter gauge extension

Backrest rail

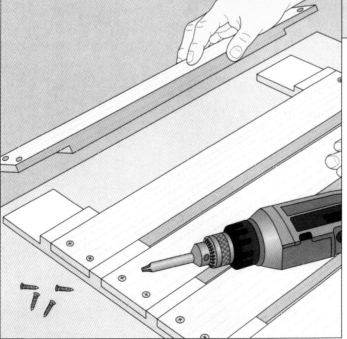

2 Attaching the slats to the rails. Drill two clearance holes at each end of every slat, then spread glue in the rabbets and dadoes of the backrest rails. Set the rails face up on a work surface and install the slats with screws *(left)*, making sure their ends are flush with the outside edges of the rails.

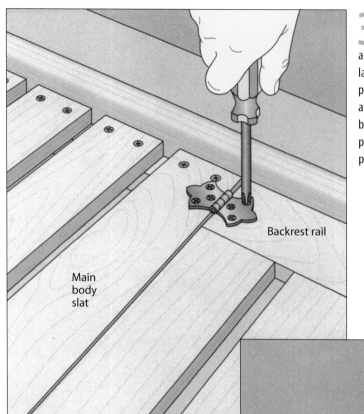

3 Attaching the backrest to the main body.
Set the backrest on the side rail cleats, leaving a 3/16-inch gap between the backrest and the last slat at the top end of the main body. Then position two butt hinges across the seam—one at each end—centering the hinge pin on the gap between the pieces. Mark the screw holes, drill a pilot hole at each mark, and screw the hinges in place *(left)*.

Backrest rail

Main body slat

4 Installing the racks. Make the two racks from lengths of 1 1/4-inch-square stock. Starting about 2 1/2 inches from one end, cut a series of notches along the top edge of each rack on your band saw. The notches should be 3/4 inch deep, angled at 45°, and spaced about 2 inches apart. Mount the racks by first fastening spacers the same width and thickness as the cleats to the side rails directly below the cleats *(see anatomy, page 46)*. Then glue and screw the racks to the spacers, aligning the top edge of each strip with the bottom edge of the cleat *(right)*. Finally, attach the backrest support stops to the top edge of the racks, flush with the back ends.

Side rail

Cleat

Rack

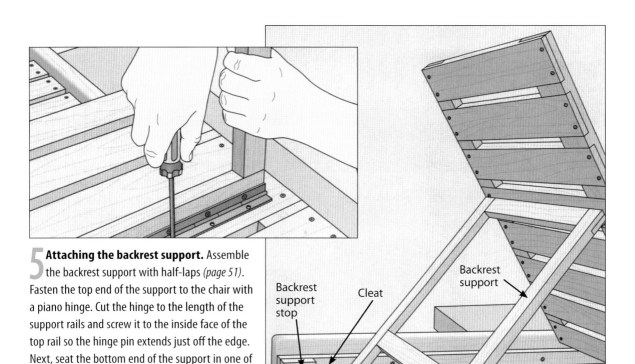

5 **Attaching the backrest support.** Assemble the backrest support with half-laps *(page 51)*. Fasten the top end of the support to the chair with a piano hinge. Cut the hinge to the length of the support rails and screw it to the inside face of the top rail so the hinge pin extends just off the edge. Next, seat the bottom end of the support in one of the rack notches and tilt up both the support and backrest so the free piano hinge leaf is centered on the fifth slat from the bottom of the backrest *(right)*. Mark the screw holes and drill a pilot hole in the slat at each mark. Turn the chair over and screw the hinge to the slat *(inset)*.

Backrest support stop

Cleat

Backrest support

Spacer

Installing the Legs

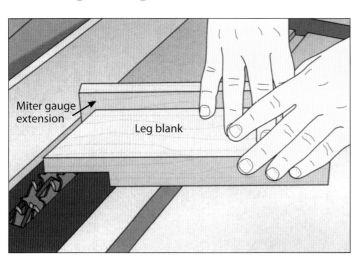

Miter gauge extension

Leg blank

1 **Preparing the legs for the side rails.** The legs are attached to the side rails with rabbets cut on a table saw fitted with a miter gauge extension and a dado head adjusted to maximum width. Set the cutting height at one-half the leg thickness and angle the miter gauge to 45°. Position the rip fence for a 3-inch cutting width. Start by sawing the rabbet shoulder, holding the stock flush against the fence and miter gauge extension. Then make a series of passes to remove the remaining waste *(left)*. Once all four legs are rabbeted, cut the curve at their bottom ends on your band saw. Keep in mind that the rear legs are 1¾ inches shorter than the front ones to enable the wheels to contact the ground.

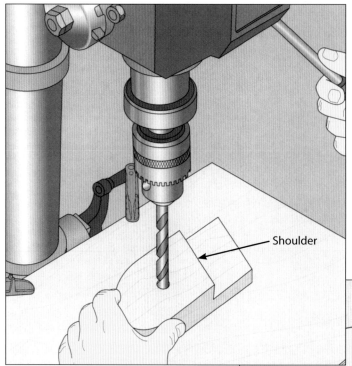

Preparing the rear legs for the wheel axles. Mark an axle hole on one of the rear legs 1⅞ inches below the rabbet shoulder. Then, install a ½-inch bit in your drill press and clamp a backup board to the machine table. Hold the leg very firmly as you drill the hole *(left)*. To ensure that the hole in the leg on the opposite side of the chair will be in exactly the same location, align the two legs face to face and slip a pencil through the hole to mark the position of the hole in the second leg.

Shoulder

Fastening the legs to the side rails. Drill two clearance holes through the rabbet in each leg and spread glue on the joint. Screw the legs in place 18 inches from the ends of the rails. Drive the screws with the leg clamped in position so the rabbet cheek remains flush against the face of the side rail and the shoulder butts against the bottom edge of the rail *(right)*. Repeat for the front legs.

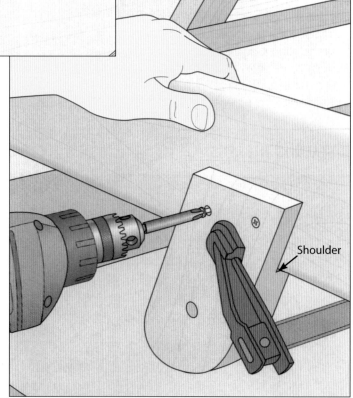

Shoulder

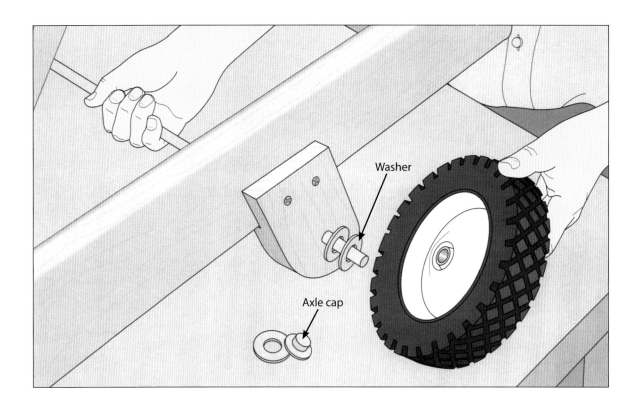

Washer

Axle cap

Axle cap

4 **Installing the wheels.** Fit the axle rods through the holes in the legs, then slip a washer and a wheel onto the axle alongside one leg. More than one washer may be necessary to enable the wheel to turn freely *(above)*. Add another washer on the outside of the wheel, then tap on an axle cap until it is snug *(left)*. Install the wheel on the opposite side of the chair the same way, but before tapping on the axle cap, cut the rod so it extends ½ inch beyond the wheel. Then install the cap.

BENCHES

The pleasures of a backyard or flower garden are meant to be shared. While a lone chair may be suited to solitary reflection, benches call out for company. More than anything, a bench is an invitation, beckoning visitors to sit and chat or simply enjoy the surrounding views.

This chapter shows how to build three different styles of benches. The garden bench shown at left and on the following pages will suit more formal tastes. Its solid, upright backrest puts it in character in a well-ordered garden. But in the right location, the bench could also serve as an interesting counterpoint to a more informal layout. In either case, try to situate it in front of tall flowers or shrubs, which will serve as a backdrop to frame the piece.

The park bench *(page 66)* is a versatile piece. The curved lines of its armrests and legs give it a more casual look than the garden bench. A simple and attractive bench when used by itself, it can be transformed into a glider when combined with the base shown on page 114. The park bench is relatively simple to make,

assembled with butt joints that are reinforced by screws. The joinery is more than sufficiently strong, and eliminates the risk that the connecting parts of the bench will trap water that could rot the wood.

Perhaps more than any other piece shown in this book, the tree bench *(page 72)* must harmonize with its setting—both in its color and size. Ideally, it should appear to be almost an organic outgrowth of its environment. Made by encircling a tree trunk with six modular seats that are attached end to end, the bench must be planned and designed with a particular tree in mind. The internal diameter of the bench should exceed that of the trunk by about 6 inches. The table on page 73 will help you choose the appropriate dimensions for your bench, given the circumference of your tree.

Before you paint your outdoor furniture, consider where it will be placed in the garden. The white of the garden bench shown at left serves as an eye-catching counterpoint to the colorful flower bed behind it.

Rather than trying the painfully difficult task of cutting all the legs of the tree bench to fit uneven ground around a tree trunk, level it using flat rocks as wedges.

Garden Bench

The garden bench is a sophisticated piece of furniture. Building it demands as much precision and attention to detail as any indoor project. It also incorporates features that give it the needed strength and durability to face the elements. The bottom ends of the arm support and back slats, for example, are housed in dadoes that extend right through the rails, allowing any moisture to drain out.

To make the bench, start by assembling the legs and rails, then add the arms and their slats, forming the two end units. Next, install the longer pieces that bridge the ends, such as the front seat rail and back rails. Finally, finish the seat and back.

To ensure that all the surfaces of the bench are uniformly smooth when the time comes to apply a finish, sand the pieces before fastening them in place.

Anatomy of a Garden Bench

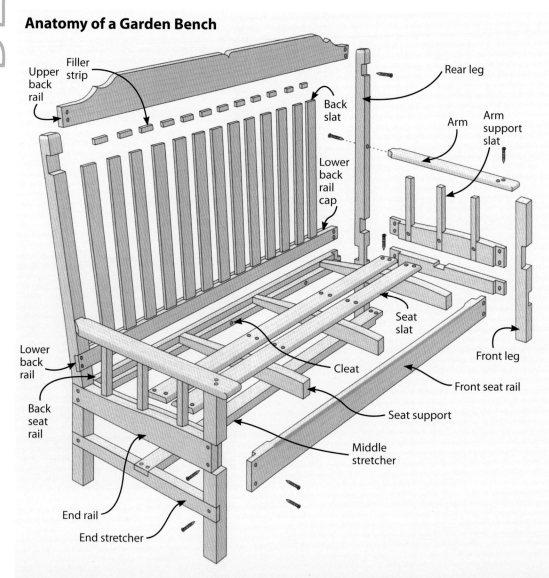

Upper back rail
Filler strip
Rear leg
Back slat
Arm
Arm support slat
Lower back rail cap
Seat slat
Lower back rail
Front leg
Back seat rail
Cleat
Front seat rail
Seat support
Middle stretcher
End rail
End stretcher

Rear Leg-and-Rail Assembly

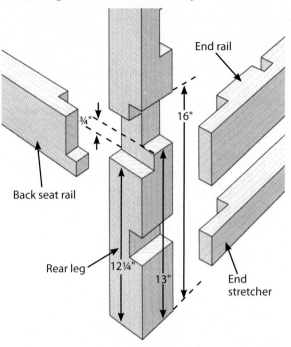

Front Leg-and-Rail Assembly

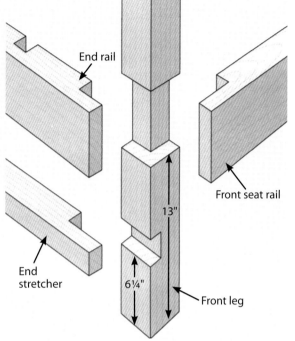

Cutting List	Qty	T	W	L
Front legs	2	1¾"	1¾"	24"
Rear legs	2	1¾"	1¾"	47¾"*
End rails	2	1¼"	4"	23⅜"
Arms	2	¾"	3"	24½"
Arm support slats	6	¾"	¾"	11¼"
Middle stretcher	1	1¼"	2¼"	60"
End stretchers	2	1¼"	2"	24"
Front seat rail	1	1¼"	4"	60"
Back seat rail	1	1¼"	3"	60"
Cleats	2	1"	1"	56½"
Seat supports	4	1¼"	2¼"	21⅛"
Seat Slats	7	1¼"	3"	57¼"
Upper back rail	1	1¼"	4¾"	60"
Lower back rail	1	1"	2¼"	60"
Lower back rail cap	1	⅜"	2¼"	56⅝"
Back slats	13	⅜"	2"	25½"

*Final Measurement. Stock should be wider to accommodate curve of leg.

Cutting Patterns for Curved Parts of Bench

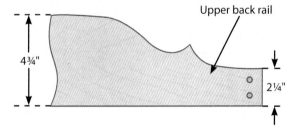

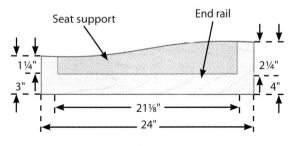

Building a Garden Bench

A dado head on a table saw cuts a dado in the front leg of a garden bench. Each front leg needs three dadoes—two on the outside face that match rabbets sawn into the end and stretcher rails, and one on the front edge for a rabbet in the front seat rail. In the setup shown at right, stop blocks clamped to a miter gauge extension ensure that the dadoes in the two legs will be in exactly the same locations.

Assembling the End Units

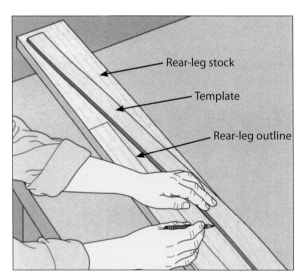

Rear-leg stock

Template

Rear-leg outline

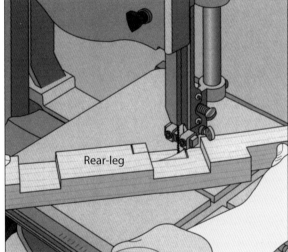

Rear-leg

1 Making the rear legs. Referring to the anatomy illustration and cutting list on the preceding pages, cut the arms, arm support slats, and the end and stretcher rails. To outline the curved rear legs on the stock, start by making a plywood or hardboard template; the legs are vertical from their bottom ends to the seat and then curve backward at about 10°, an angle that most users will find comfortable. Once the template is ready, trace its outline on the leg stock with a pencil. Using a 2-by-6 will enable you to use the same blank for both legs *(above)*. Cut the legs on your band saw.

2 Cutting the half-lap joints. All of the dadoes and rabbets for the half-laps used to assemble the end units can be cut on the table saw *(photo, above)*—except for those on the back edges of the rear legs for the back seat rail. These are cut on a band saw because the cuts are located on the inside of the leg curves, and the stock cannot rest flat on a table saw table at these points. Start by making all the table saw cuts, then outline the remaining dado on each rear leg. Feeding the stock into the blade with both hands, cut the sides of the dado with two cross-grain cuts, then make a series of curved *(above)* and straight cuts to remove the remaining waste.

3 **Attaching the end and stretcher rails to the legs.** Set front and rear legs from the same side of the bench outside face up on a work surface and apply waterproof glue in the dadoes. Tap the end and stretcher rails in position, check the unit for square and drill pilot holes in the rails, two at each end of the end rail and one into the stretcher rail. Screw the pieces together *(right).*

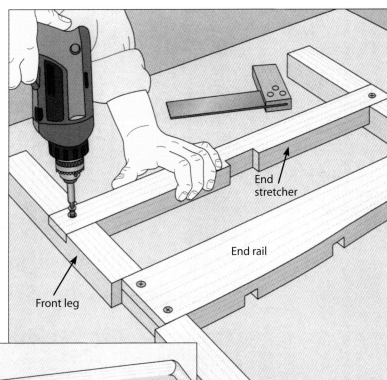

End stretcher

End rail

Front leg

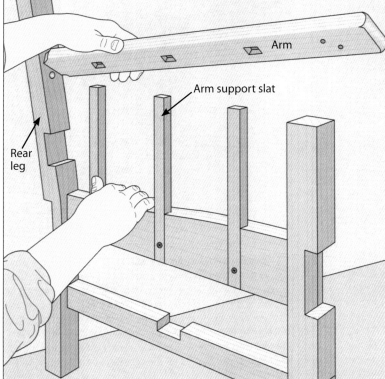

Arm

Arm support slat

Rear leg

4 **Installing the arms.** Screw the arm support slats to the end rails, making certain that the supports' bottom ends are flush with the bottom edges of the rails. Then, holding one leg assembly upright, set the arm in position, centering it on the supports and butting the back end against the rear leg. Outline the supports on the underside of the arm and cut a ¼-inch-deep mortise into the arm within each outline. Also bore two clearance holes through the arm in line with the front leg and through the rear leg into the end of the arm. Next, spread some glue in the arm mortises and at the points where the arm contacts the legs, fit the arm in position again *(left),* and screw it to the legs.

Attaching the Seat Rails and Middle Stretcher

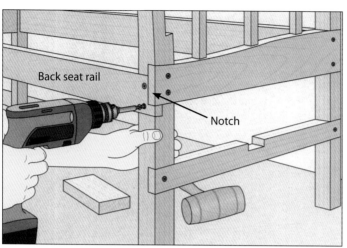

Back seat rail

Notch

1 Installing the seat rails. Start by attaching the front seat rail to the front legs, using a mallet and wood block to tap the half-laps together, and glue and screws to fix the pieces. For the back rail, set the assembly upright on a work surface, position the board against the rear legs, and mark the position of the notch that must be cut in the end to enable the outside face of the rail to sit flush with the back edges of the legs. Cut the notch, then glue and screw the rail to the legs *(left)*.

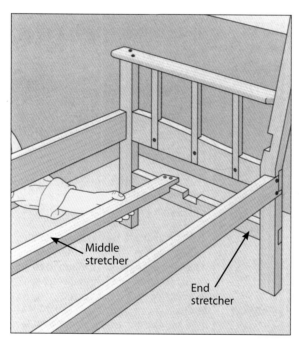

Middle stretcher

End stretcher

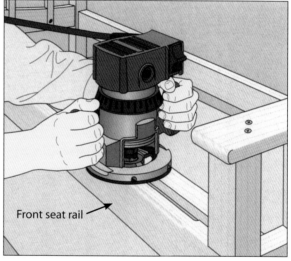

Front seat rail

2 Attaching the middle stretcher. Cut a rabbet at each end of the stretcher to mate with the dadoes in the end stretchers. Drill two clearance holes through the stretcher at each end of the board, then spread some glue in the rabbets, set the piece in position *(above)*, and screw it down.

3 Rounding over the front seat rail. To make the bench more comfortable, round over the top edge of the front seat rail. Install a piloted rounding-over bit in a router and set the depth of cut to reach your final depth in two passes. Make the first pass along the inside face of the rail. Butting the router base plate against one front leg and holding the tool level on the rail, feed the bit into the stock and along the rail *(above)*; make sure the bit's pilot bearing is pressed against the stock throughout. Stop the cut when the router contacts the opposite front leg, then repeat the pass along the rail's front face. Increase the cutting depth and make two more passes.

Installing the Seat

1 Attaching the cleats and seat supports. Secure the cleats to the seat rails with glue and screws spaced at 8-inch intervals; position the cleats so that the top edges of the seat supports and seat rails lie flush. With the cleats in position, set the bench on its back and attach the end seat supports to the cleats, driving the screws from underneath; the supports should be flush against the legs and end rails. Next, fasten the middle seat supports to the cleats, spacing them evenly and holding each piece in position as you drive the screws *(right)*.

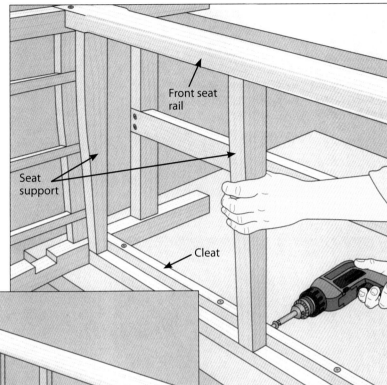

Front seat rail

Seat support

Cleat

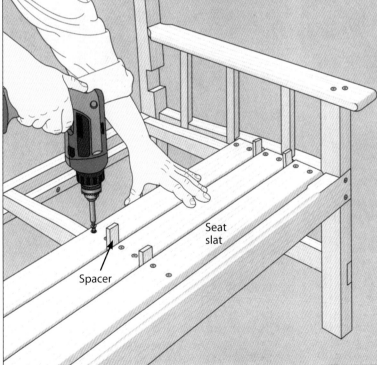

Seat slat

Spacer

2 Installing the seat slats. Round over the top edges of the seat slats and test-fit them in the bench so that there is ¼-inch gap between them; trim the slats' edges, if necessary. Mark the locations of the seat supports on each slat and drill two clearance holes through the slats at each mark. Starting at the front seat rail, screw the slats to the supports, using ¼-inch spacers to maintain the gap between the pieces *(left)*.

Assembling the Back

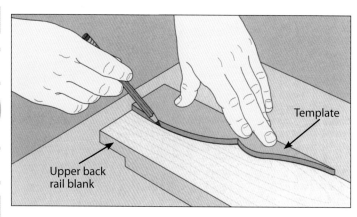

Upper back rail blank

Template

1 **Shaping the upper back rail.** Cut the upper back rail to size, then saw the rabbets at its ends. Outline the curve along the rail's top edge using a template based on the pattern illustrated on page 59. Align the template with the top corner of the rail at one end and mark its outline with a pencil *(left)*. Repeat at the other end, then cut away the waste on your band saw.

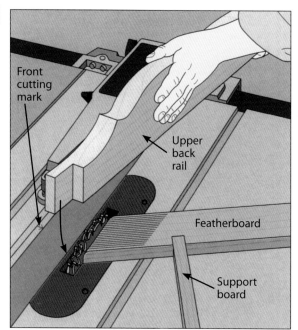

Front cutting mark

Upper back rail

Featherboard

Support board

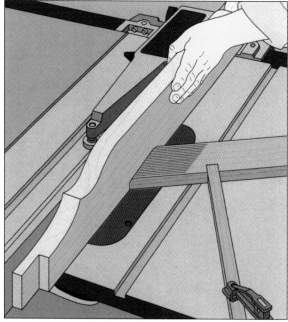

2 **Preparing the rail for the back slats.** Cut the groove for the slats along the rail on your table saw equipped with a dado head. Adjust the width of the blades to the slat thickness—⅜ inch—and the cutting height to 1 inch. Center the rail over the blades and butt the rip fence against the stock. To help keep the rail pressed against the fence, clamp a featherboard to the saw table, braced by a support board installed at a 90° angle; round over the top edge of the featherboard to facilitate lowering the workpiece onto

the blades. To help you determine the position of the dado head when it is hidden by the rail during the cut, mark two lines on the fence at the point where the blades start and stop cutting. Holding the rail against the fence just above the blades and aligning the front end of the piece with the cutting mark on the fence, slowly lower it onto the head *(above, left)*. Once the rail is sitting squarely on the table, feed it forward while pressing it against the fence *(above, right)*. Stop the cut once the back end of the rail reaches the back cutting mark.

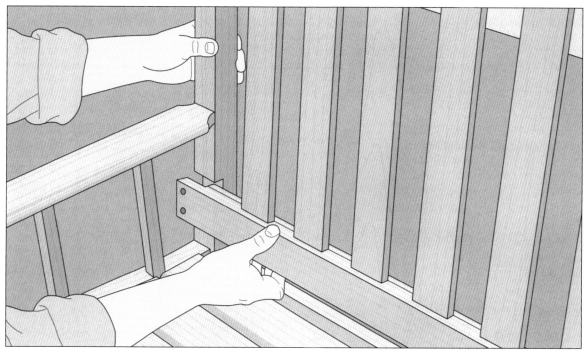

3 Fastening the lower back rail to the rear legs. Prepare the lower back rail and then install the back slats in the rail, proceeding as you would for a porch swing *(page 106)*. Spread some glue on the contacting surfaces of the lower rail and rear legs, fit the assemblies together, *(above)* and drive two screws into each end of the rail.

4 Attaching the upper back rail. Positioning the upper rail over the slats, start at one end to push the rail down, snapping the slats into the groove as you go. Once the pieces are all in place, glue and screw the half-laps joining the rail and rear legs *(left)*. To complete the bench, glue wood filler strips in the upper rail groove between the slats. This will keep the slats from shifting.

Park Bench

The park bench is a cozy seat for two. It can serve as a stationary bench, as shown here, or as a glider, using the base shown on page 114. The height of the bench without the glider may be a bit low for some users, but adding 3 inches to the leg lengths provided in the cutting list will yield a standard-height bench. Using mainly simple butt joints, the park bench is relatively straightforward to construct. While not as strong as the half-lap, the butt joint is quick and easy to assemble—and it does an even better job of shedding water and moisture. Reinforcing the joints with waterproof glue and screws makes them sufficiently strong.

Another concession to simplicity is the use of same-size stock for back and seat slats. This enables you rip all the slats with the same setting on your table saw, speeding construction and reducing errors.

Anatomy of a Park Bench

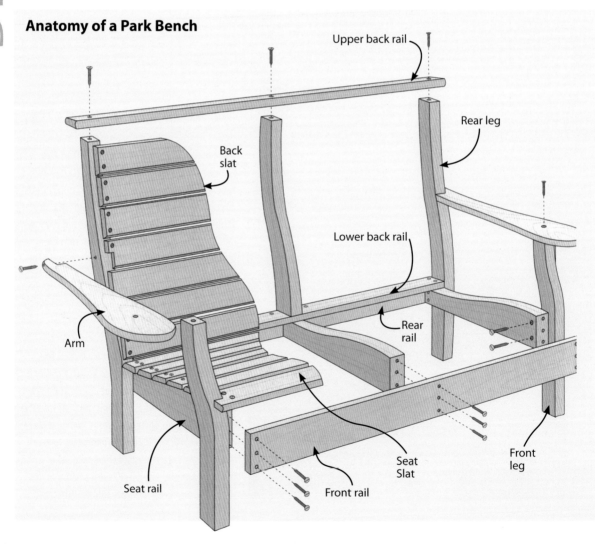

Upper back rail

Rear leg

Back slat

Lower back rail

Rear rail

Arm

Seat Slat

Front leg

Seat rail

Front rail

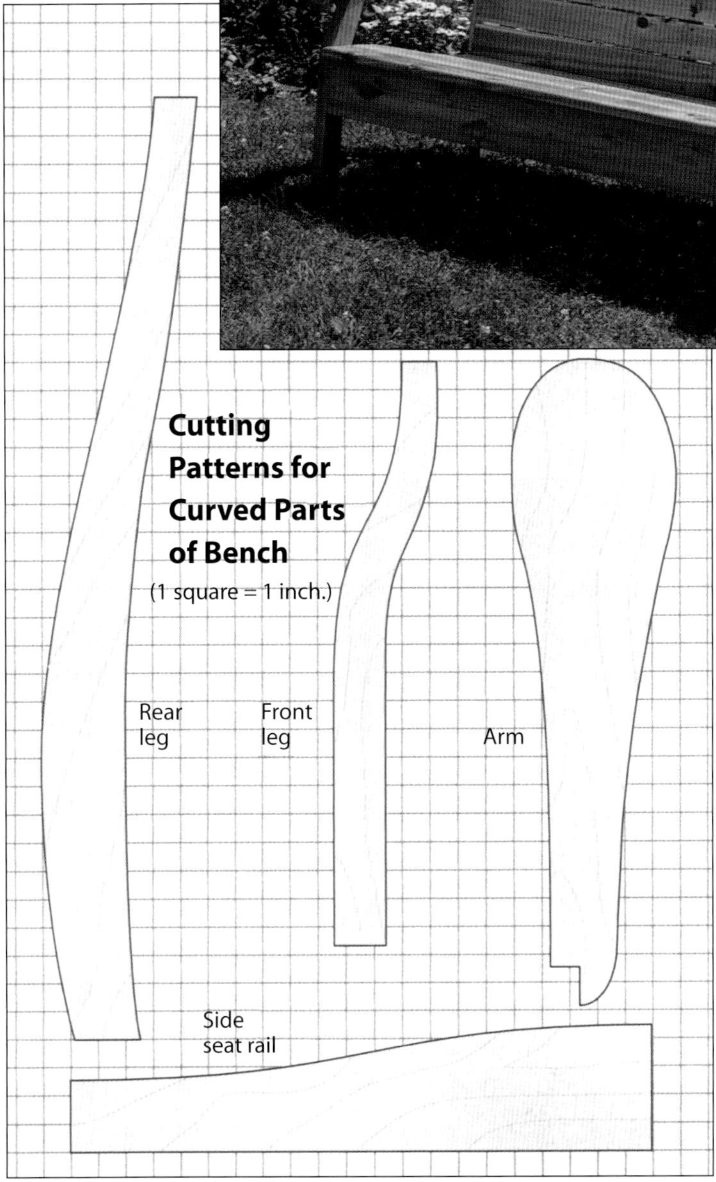

Cutting Patterns for Curved Parts of Bench

(1 square = 1 inch.)

Rear leg

Front leg

Arm

Side seat rail

Two coats of spar varnish applied on the park bench shown at right bring out the rich natural tones of the wood—in this case, Northern white cedar.

Cutting List	Qty	Th	W	L
Front legs	2	1¼"	4"	20¾"
Rear legs	3	1¼"	5"	33⅜"
Seat rails	3	1¼"	4¾"	21"
Arms	2	¾"	6"	23"
Front rail	1	¾"	4¾"	46"
Rear rails	2	¾"	2¾"	46"
Upper back rail	1	¾"	2"	49¼"
Seat slats	6	¾"	3"	47"
Back slats	7	¾"	3"	47"

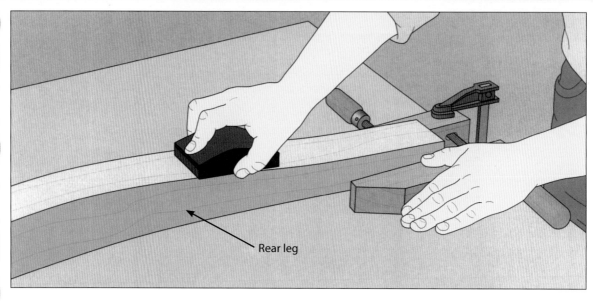

Rear leg

Making the End Units

1 Shaping the legs. Start building the bench by assembling the end units, which consist of the seat and seat rails. Referring to the cutting patterns shown on page 67, make templates for the front and rear legs. Then trace the designs onto your leg stock *(page 60)* and cut out the legs on the band saw. Smooth the surfaces of each leg with a sanding block *(above)*, securing the stock to a work surface and sanding with the grain. Rearrange the leg in the clamps as necessary.

2 Attaching the seat rails to the legs. Cut the seat rails to size, then fasten one to each leg. Mark layout lines on the legs to position the rail properly: The rail should be inset from the outside edges of the legs by ¾ inch to allow the front and rear rails to be set flush with the leg's edges; the bottom edge of the seat rail should be 5¾ inches from the bottom of the rear leg and 6 inches from the bottom of the front leg. Spread some glue on the contacting surfaces of the pieces, align the rail with your layout lines, and use a try square as you fasten the rails to the legs to ensure that the bottom edge of the rails remains perpendicular to the outside edge of each leg *(right)*.

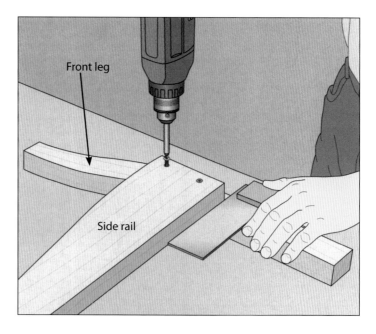

Front leg

Side rail

Assembling the Seat

1 Installing the front and rear rails. Cut the front and rear rails to size and drill clearance holes at the ends of each piece. Using glue and screws, fasten the rear rail in place; drive one screw at each end to start, check for square, then install the remaining fasteners. Install the front rail the same way *(right)*, then attach the third seat rail to the front and rear rails, centering it between the end units.

Park Bench

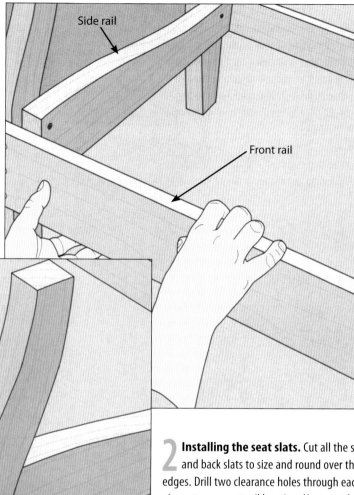

Side rail

Front rail

2 Installing the seat slats. Cut all the seat and back slats to size and round over their edges. Drill two clearance holes through each piece at every seat rail location. Next, notch the first seat slat at the front of the bench to fit around the front legs. To ensure the slat sits flush against the curved front edge of the legs, hold it in position on the rails, outline the leg profile at each end with a pencil *(left)* and trim to the line with a chisel. Screw the slats in place, separating them with ¼-inch spacers *(page 63)*.

Installing the Arm

1 Shaping the arm. Outline the appropriate cutting pattern *(page 67)* on one arm blank, then cut the notch at the back end of the blank that will enable the arm to fit around the rear leg. To ensure the inside surfaces of the arm and rear leg will align, hold the blank in position and mark a line along the top face of the blank that parallels the leg's inside face *(right)*. Cut the arm to shape on your band saw, then use a router to round over all its edges, except for those that define the notch. Use the first arm to outline the opposite one.

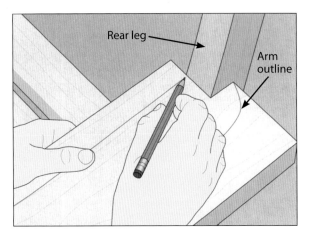

Rear leg

Arm outline

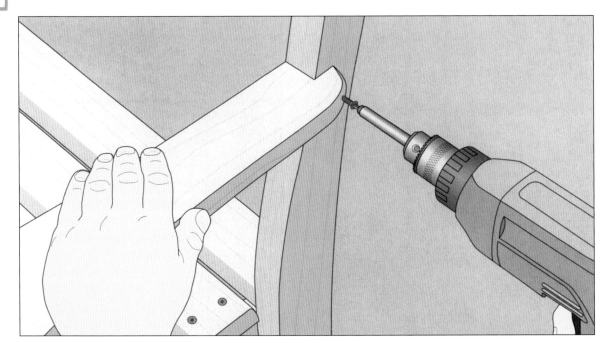

2 Installing the arms. Position the arm on the bench so that the inside edge is flush with the rear leg and overhangs the inside face of the front leg by 1¼ inches. Mark location lines on the underside of the arm and drill clearance holes through it. Then apply glue to the contacting surfaces of the arm and legs and fasten each arm in place *(above)*.

Assembling the Back

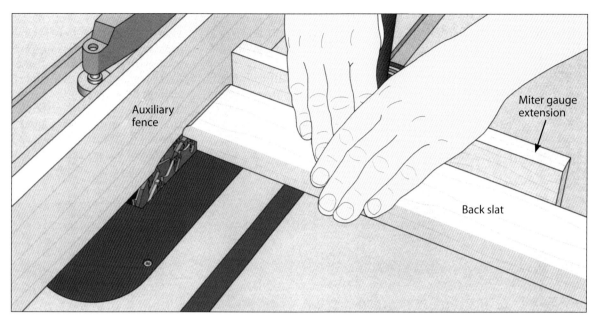

Auxiliary
fence

Miter gauge
extension

Back slat

1 **Rabbeting the back slats.** Cut the rabbets at the ends of the back slats on your table saw. Install a dado head and adjust its width to slightly more than ½ inch. Then attach an auxiliary fence, position the fence for a ½-inch cutting width, and raise the blades into the wooden fence to notch it, making sure that the dado head is clear of the metal one. Adjust the cutting height to one-half the slat thickness and screw an extension board to the miter gauge. Feed the slats rounded-over side up, holding the stock flush against the fence and miter gauge extension while you make the cut *(above)*.

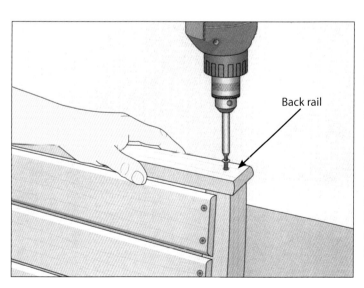

Back rail

2 **Attaching back slats and rail.** Using glue and two screws at each end, fasten the back slats to the rear legs; cut ¹⁄₁₆-inch spacers to maintain the proper gap between the bottommost back slat and the seat, and ¼-inch spacers for the remaining rows. Before applying glue to the fourth slat from the bottom, notch it at each end to fit around the arms. Once all the back slats are installed, use two screws to fasten the bottom end of the back support piece to the seat slat at the back of the bench. Complete the bench by installing the upper back rail. Apply glue to the contacting surfaces of the rail and legs, then screw the support in position *(left)*.

Tree Bench

Once installed, a tree bench can become an integral part of its environment, appearing as natural, necessary, and stable as the tree it encircles. Indeed, this bench is by definition a custom-made project. You cannot complete the cutting list until you measure the circumference of the tree around which the bench will fit. Refer to the chart opposite to help you size the variable parts of your project. Although final assembly of the bench is done on site, you will avoid frustration

if you first test-assemble the six identical seating units in the shop. Once you are satisfied with the fit, disassemble the bench only partially to move it. Remove the cap rail, seat, slats, back slats, and apron from two opposite sections, leaving two pairs of seat sections intact. When you reach your tree, position the two intact sections around the trunk, then reattach the removed sections. Finally, apply a waterproof sealer to protect the wood from weather.

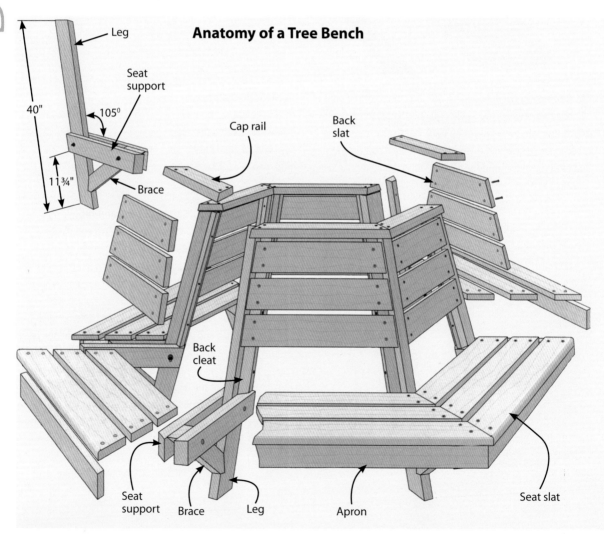

Anatomy of a Tree Bench

Leg

Seat support

40"

105°

11¾"

Brace

Cap rail

Back slat

Back cleat

Seat support

Brace

Leg

Apron

Seat slat

Wrapped around the trunk of a stately ash tree, a six-sided tree bench offers a shady place to sit and reflect. Its design allows one to view the entire panorama without moving the bench; the user need only shift to another seat. The bench shown at right was finished with a green stain, enabling it to blend unobtrusively with its surroundings.

Cutting List	Qty	T	W	L
Legs	6	1⅜"	3⅝"	40"
Braces	6	1⅜"	3"	16¾"
Seat supports	12	1⅜"	3⅝"	17¾"
Back cleats	12	1½"	1½"	25"
Cap rails	6	1⅝"	3½"	*
Aprons	6	1⅜"	3½"	*
Back slats	18	1¼"	5"	*
Seat slats	18	1¼"	5"	*
Carriage bolts	12	x	⁵⁄₁₆" diam.	5"

Tree Circumference	Inside Length Cap Rail*	Tree Circumference	Inside Length Cap Rail*	Tree Circumference	Inside Length Cap Rail*
50"	12¾"	72"	16¾"	94"	20¾"
52"	13"	74"	17¼"	96"	21¼"
54"	13½"	76"	17½"	98"	21½"
56"	13¾"	78"	17⅞"	100"	21⅞"
58"	14"	80"	18¼"	102"	22¼"
60"	14½"	82"	18⅝"	104"	22⅝"
62"	14⅞"	84"	19"	106"	23"
64"	15¼"	86"	19⅜"	108"	23⅜"
66"	15⅝"	88"	19¾"	110"	23¾"
68"	16"	90"	20"	112"	24½"
70"	16⅜"	92"	20⅜"		* Rounded up to nearest ⅛ inch

Calculating the dimensions of a tree bench. The size of some tree bench parts—the cap rails, aprons, and slats—depend on the circumference of the tree. Since the mitered cap rails hug the tree closest, their length along the inside (or shorter) edges is critical. Ideally, there should be a 1½-inch gap between the cap rails and the tree at the midpoint of each rail. Start by measuring the tree's circumference (simply wrap a measuring tape around the trunk at the cap rail

height) and round your result up to one of the dimensions in the chart above. The same line on the chart will give you the required length of the cap rails along their inside edges. Cut the length of the other variable pieces—the aprons and slats—to fit.

If the tree circumference is less than 50 inches, use 12¾-inch-long cap rails. If it exceeds 112 inches, you will need to build an octagonal bench—or find a smaller tree.

Building a Tree Bench

A tree bench back slat is trimmed to length with a compound miter cut on a table saw. In the setup shown at right, the blade is angled to 30° so that the ends of the slat will sit flush against the adjoining legs; the miter gauge angle is set to match the splay angle—or side-to-side slope—of the legs. To help prevent kickback, the workpiece is clamped to a miter gauge extension and the cut is set up with the waste piece to the right of the blade.

Making the Support Assemblies

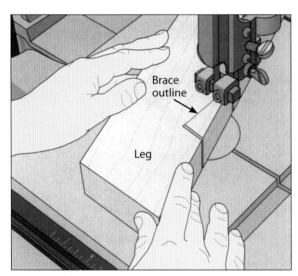

Brace outline

Leg

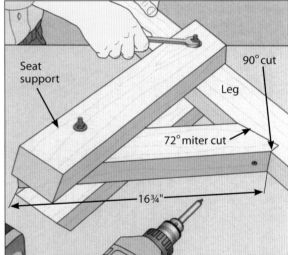

Seat support

90° cut

Leg

72° miter cut

16¾"

1 Assembling the legs, braces and seat supports.
Start by making the six support assemblies; each one comprises a leg and brace and two seat supports. Miter both ends of each leg at a 75° angle. Miter the bottom end of the brace at a 72° angle, then trim the bottom corner with a cut at a 90° angle to the miter cut; this second cut should intersect the end of the brace 3¼ inches from the top edge. Make a 45° miter cut at the other end of the brace so that the board measures 16¾ inches along its bottom edge. Holding the brace at a 105° angle to the leg 4 inches from the leg's bottom end, outline the bottom end of the brace on the face

of the leg. Then cut out the marked notch on your band saw (above, left). Next, use glue and a screw to fasten the brace to the leg, driving the fastener through the brace's bottom edge. Now cut the seat supports to length, beveling the front ends at 30°. The back end of each support should be flush with the leg's back edge and the support's top edge should be flush with the top end of the brace. Clamp the supports in position on the leg and brace, and mark a hole at each end of both supports for a ⁵⁄₁₆-inch-diameter carriage bolt. Drill the holes and install the bolts, washers and nuts, tightening with a wrench (above, right).

2 **Preparing the back cleats.** Make the 12 back cleats from lengths of 1½-by-1½-inch stock. Rip both edges of each piece at a 30° angle so the narrow face of the cleat is ¾ inch wide. Cut the bottom end of the cleat so it will sit flat on the seat support with the wide face flush against the leg. To trim the top end of the cleat, hold it in position against the seat support and leg, mark your cutting line along the leg's top end *(right)*, and make the cut on the band saw.

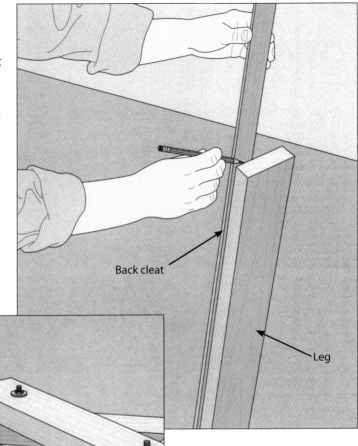

Back cleat

Leg

3 **Attaching the cleats to the legs.** To offset the cleats from the front edge of the legs by the required 1¾ inches, make a ⁵⁄₁₆-inch-thick spacer that you can use to space the cleat from the leg's back edge. Drill three clearance holes through the cleat and, using glue to bond the cleat to the leg, fasten the cleat in place. Hold the spacer against the cleat and flush with the leg's back edge as you drive the screws *(left)*.

Spacer

Joining the Support Assemblies

1 Installing the cap rails. Cut the cap rails to length, mitering the ends at 60° and beveling the front edge at 70°. (Refer to the chart on page 73 to determine the length of the rail along its inside edge.) Drill two clearance holes through the rails at each end. Then prop up two support assemblies and mark a line along the top end of each leg that divides its thickness in half. Align the ends of the cap rail with the marked lines and fasten the piece to the legs *(right)*. Now add on another cap rail and support assembly, continuing until all six of each are installed.

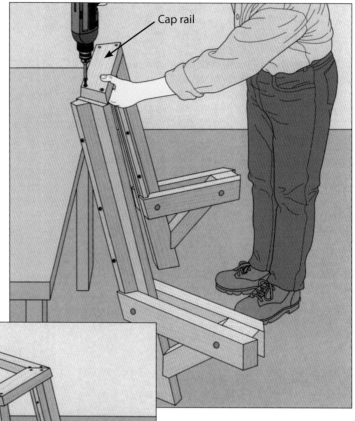

Cap rail

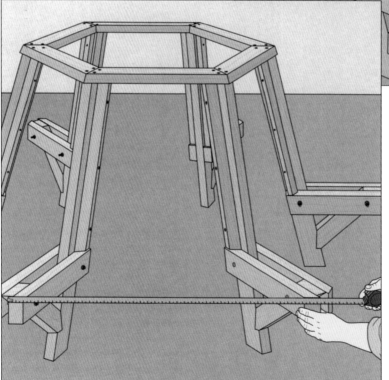

2 Spacing the support assemblies. Once all the cap rails are in place, set the legs upright on the shop floor and check whether the support assemblies are evenly spaced. Making sure the ends of all the legs are flat on the floor, measure from the inside face of one right-hand side seat support to the inside face of the adjoining piece. Repeat with the remaining supports and gently nudge the legs to one side or the other, if necessary, until all your measurements are equal *(left)*. This may take some trial and error.

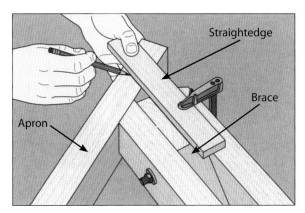

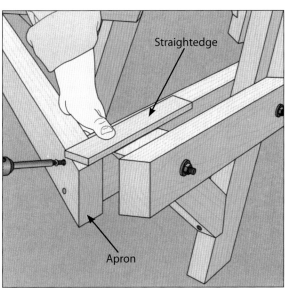

3 Sizing the aprons. You will need to mark one apron in position to determine the final length of the pieces. Start by cutting the aprons about 36 inches longer than the cap rails. Next, mark lines along the top ends of two adjoining braces that divide their thickness in half, and clamp a wood strip as a straightedge along each marked line. To mark the apron, work with a helper to hold the board in position at each end; making sure the apron is flush against the seat supports and butted against the underside of the straightedges, run a pencil along the wood strip at each end of the apron *(above)*. Trim the apron, then use the piece to mark the remaining ones.

4 Attaching the aprons. Drill a pair of clearance holes at each end of the aprons. Using straightedges to center the ends of the pieces across the braces, screw the aprons in place *(above)*. You may need a helper to hold up the opposite end of each apron as you drive the first pair of screws.

Installing Seat and Back Slats

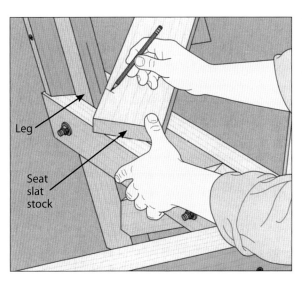

1 Marking the first seat slat. Start sizing the seat slats at the back of the bench. To determine the exact angle at which you will need to miter the ends of the slats, hold the first blank in position on the seat supports and against the legs and use a sliding bevel to measure the angle formed by the slat and one leg. Adjust the miter gauge on your table saw to this angle. To locate your cutting lines on the board, mark lines along the front edges of the legs that divide their thickness in half. Then, with the slat blank in position, draw the cutting marks ⅛ inch inside those on the legs *(left)*. This will leave the required ¼-gap between slats. Trim the slat to length and use it to size the remaining ones. Then fasten the slats to the seat supports with two screws at each end, leaving a ¼-gap between the pieces.

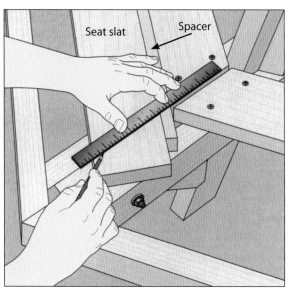

Seat slat

Spacer

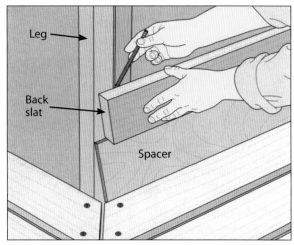

Leg

Back slat

Spacer

2 Attaching the remaining seat slats. The second and third rows of the seat slats are installed in much the same way as the first. To mark each slat, set it on the seat supports and butt it edge to edge against the first slat, placing a ¾-inch-thick spacer stick between the slats. Then use a pencil and a rule to mark lines across the face of the slat that align with the ends of the first slat *(above)*. Miter the slat and fasten it to the seat supports, maintaining the ¼-inch gap between the ends and a ¾-inch space between edges.

3 Trimming the back slats to length. The ends of the back slats must be cut at a compound angle—both mitered and beveled—so they sit flush against the legs of the tree bench. To mark the slats, set a 6½-inch-wide spacer on edge on the first seat slat and place the back slat blank on the spacer. Holding the slat flat against two adjoining legs, run a pencil along the inside face of the each leg to mark cutting lines on the face of the slat *(above)*. To cut the compound angle on your table saw, angle the blade to 60° and adjust the miter gauge to the angle marked on the slat *(photo, page 74)*. Use the slat as a guide to trimming the others in the bottom tier.

4 Installing the back slats. Drill two clearance holes at each end of every back slat. Using the spacer to separate the slat from the seat slat below and a clamp to hold the slat level, fasten each piece to the back cleats *(right)*. Install the second and third tiers of back slats the same way, but use a ¾-inch-thick spacer to separate the board edges. Apply your finish before setting up the bench in its chosen location outdoors and so avoid splattering the tree with paint, stain, or varnish. Before transporting the bench, remove the cap rail, apron, and slats from two opposite sides of the assembly. This will leave two pairs of frame sections that, together with the removed pieces, are easy to move. Once the two frame sections are positioned around the tree, you an reinstall the detached boards *(photo, page 79)*.

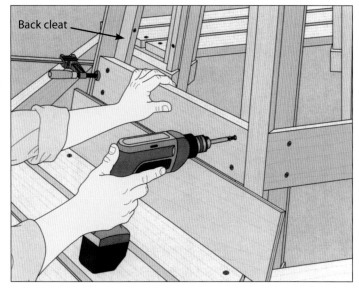

Back cleat

With two double frame sections positioned on opposite sides of an ash tree, a tree bench apron is fastened in place. Since the bench was built in the shop and disassembled for easy transport and positioning, installing the remaining pieces—the seat and back slats, the cap rails, and the last apron—is a simple matter. The boards can be fitted into position and the screws driven into their predrilled holes.

Setting up a Tree Bench

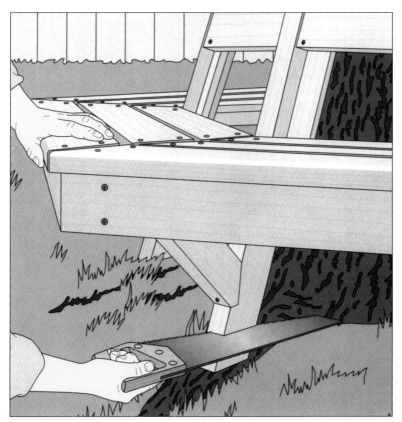

Leveling a tree bench. Once all the pieces of your tree bench have been fastened in place, work with a helper to lift it and position the assembly around the tree. The gap between the trunk and cap rails should be equal around the tree's circumference. Because the terrain is unlikely to be as level as your shop floor, one or more of the legs may not be in contact with the ground. Rotating the bench in one direction or the other may solve the problem. If not, trim a leg *(left)* that is resting on higher ground, or prop up a leg that is not touching the ground *(photo, page 57)*.

TABLES

Eating outdoors is one of life's simple pleasures. The patio table and the folding picnic table shown in this chapter are excellent additions to any outdoor furniture ensemble. The patio table *(page 82)* is large enough to seat six adults comfortably. It is, in fact, as big as many dining tables. The lattice-work grid that comprises the top gives the table a light appearance, and literally reduces the weight.

Like many pieces of outdoor furniture, the patio table relies on half-laps to join the legs and rails. The frame surrounding the lattice grid is assembled with bridle joints. These strong joints help make up for some of the rigidity sacrificed by having a lattice top instead of a solid one. The grid itself is formed by joining the strips of wood with half-lap joints. This calls for cutting hundreds of dadoes—a daunting task, but one made manageable with the help of the indexing jig shown on page 90.

The folding picnic table *(page 92)* offers a convenient solution to the need for a table that is transportable. It is designed to fold down neatly and can fit inside most car trunks. When locked in the up position, the table provides a sturdy surface large enough to seat four adults. Its construction combines the use of prefabricated parts and building to fit. While the top can be made by referring only to the cutting list *(page 92)*, the legs must be planned carefully so they nest inside each other.

A useful companion to both tables is the keyed tenon bench *(page 100)*. It is attractive, simple, and exceedingly strong. This is a very old design but it looks perfectly at home on a contemporary deck or patio. Its simple design makes it easy to build to whatever length you need. Simply change the length of the slats and stretchers listed in the cutting list as required.

The convenience of a table that folds can be a liability when it is laden with food. One way to ensure that the table does not collapse at an inopportune time is to use a butterfly catch pull to lock the leg rail and support block together.

A lattice top makes a table much lighter, but remember not to make the holes too large or glasses will spill easily. The spaces should be no larger than 1¼ inches square.

Patio Table

The patio table is a slightly formal but welcome addition to any deck or backyard. The lattice grid lends a lightness to a fairly large table. A clever design element holds the grid in place with no need to cut a surrounding rabbet. The inside length and width of the frame are 1½ inches longer than those of the table base. This creates a ¾ inch ledge to hold the grid on top of the rails, within the frame.

The grid itself can be assembled on the workbench and then installed in the table. Prepare the strips one inch longer than cited in the cutting list, cut the dadoes for the half-laps, then trim them to fit *(page 90)*.

Though delicate looking, the table is far from flimsy. But, while it will hold up to reasonable use, do not expect it to withstand the same stress as your oak dining table.

The grid of lattice strips lacks the same strength and rigidity as a solid top. To increase the top's resistance to racking, the corners are joined with bridle joints, which offer twice the gluing surface of half-laps.

The base and the lattice grid of the patio table are easy to separate, lending itself to this striking finishing technique. The lattice grid was removed as a whole unit and finished with tung oil and spar varnish. The rest of the table was stained with a dark green opaque finish, creating a contrast that highlights the lattice wood's natural color.

Cutting List	Qty	T	W	L
Legs	4	1½"	3½"	29"
Side rails	2	1¼"	4¼"	55½"
End rails	2	1¼"	4¼"	30½"
Frame sides	2	1¼"	3"	60"
Frame ends	2	1¼"	3"	36"
Short lattice strips	24	¾"	1¼"	29⅞"*
Long lattice strips	13	¾"	1¼"	54"* *prepare strips one inch longer than trim to fit after cutting dados

Anatomy of a Patio Table

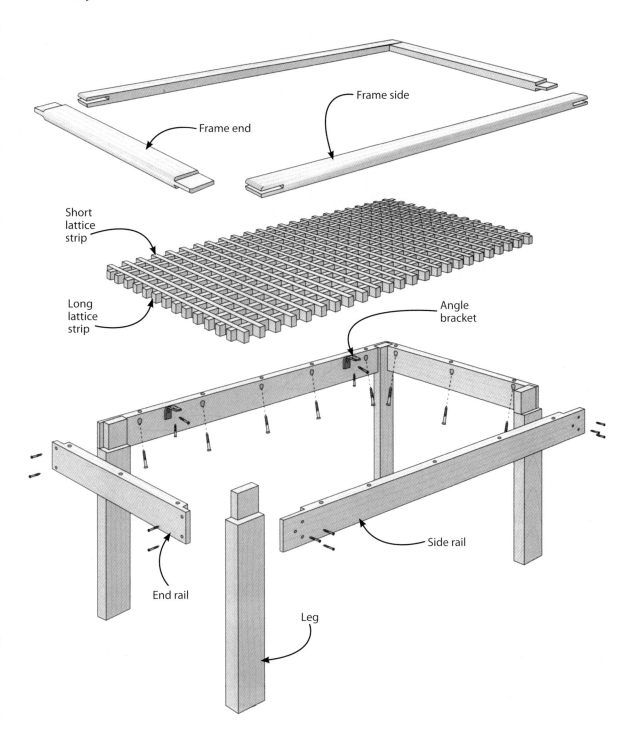

Frame end

Frame side

Short lattice strip

Long lattice strip

Angle bracket

Side rail

End rail

Leg

Assembling Legs and Stretchers

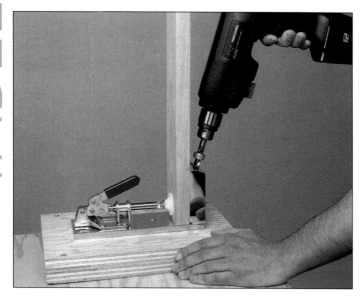

Pocket holes are an excellent choice for attaching the table frame to the rails. They can also be used to join a rail to a post. The commercial jig shown at left enables you to bore the holes with a minimum of setup time. The device clamps the workpiece in position and features a bushing that holds the drill bit at the correct angle. The combination bit shown bores a clearance hole for the screw shank and countersinks the hole for the head in one operation. A stop collar attached to the bit regulates the drilling depth.

1 Cutting the half-laps. The rails are joined to the legs with half-laps. Start with the side rails and the legs. Install a dado head on your table saw and set the cutting height to half the thickness of the stock. Adjust the fence to make a 3½-inch-long rabbet, then add an extension board to your miter gauge. Cut the rabbets in the side rails and the outside faces of the legs. Next, hold the leg on edge against the miter gauge extension and cut the dado in the outside edge to accomodate the end rail *(right)*. To prepare the end rails, shift the fence for a 1½ inch long rabbet, then make the cut on the inside face of the end rails. The final step is to trim ⅝ inch from each end of the end rails. This will allow the end rails to sit flush against the legs.

Miter gauge extension

Corner Half-Lap Joint Jig

If you have to make corner half-laps in several boards of the same size, it is worth taking the time to build the jig shown at right. Cut the two base pieces and the stop block from plywood the same thickness as your stock. The base pieces should be wide enough to accommodate the edge guides and support the router base plate as you cut the half-laps. Use solid wood strips for the four edge guides.

To assemble the jig, mark the shoulder of the half-lap on one workpiece and set the board face-up on a work surface. Butt the base pieces against the edges of the board so the shoulder mark is near the middle of the base pieces. Install a straight bit in the router and align the cutter with the shoulder mark. Position one end guide across the base pieces and against the tool's base plate. Without moving the workpiece, repeat the procedure to position the opposite guide. Now align the bit with the edges of the workpiece and attach the side guides, leaving a slight gap between the router base plate and each guide. (The first half-lap you make with the jig will rout reference grooves in the base pieces.) Slip the stop block under the end guide, butt it against the end of the workpiece, and screw it in place. Countersink all fasteners.

To use the jig, clamp it to the work surface and slide the workpiece between the base pieces until it butts against the stop block. Protecting the stock with a wood pad, clamp the workpiece

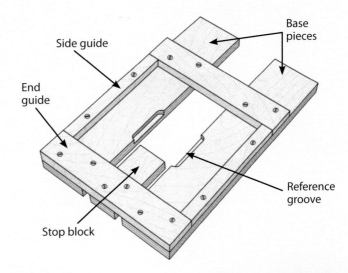

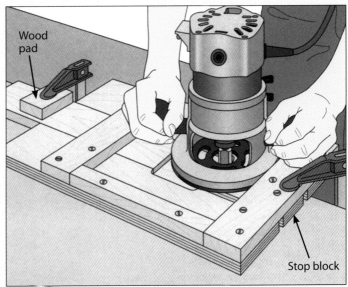

in place. Adjust the router's cutting depth to one-half the stock thickness. Then, with the router positioned inside the guides, grip the tool firmly, turn it on, and lower the bit into the workpiece. Guide the router in a clockwise direction to cut the outside edges of the half-lap, keeping the base plate flush against a guide at all times. Then rout out the remaining waste, feeding the tool against the direction of bit rotation.

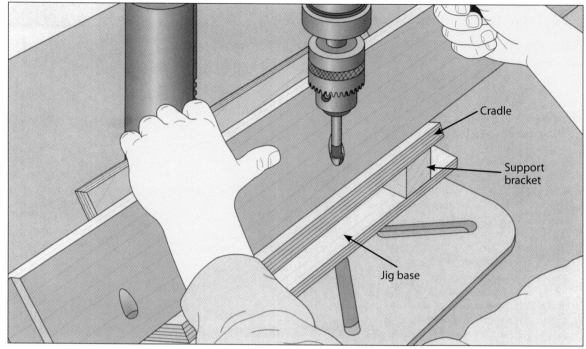

Cradle

Support bracket

Jig base

2 Making pocket holes. Use a commercial pocket hole cutter like the one shown on page 84 or a shop-built jig like the one shown above to make the pocket holes. This jig consists of two pieces of ¾-inch plywood joined to form an L-shaped cradle and two support brackets that angle the cradle at 15° from the vertical. Seat the workpiece in the cradle, and align the stock so the clearance hole will exit in the middle of the board edge. Install a Forstner bit and drill a hole just deep enough to recess the screw head *(above)*. Then install a brad-point bit and bore the clearance hole through the workpiece.

3 Attaching legs. Set one pair of legs on a work surface and apply glue to the rabbets. Slide a side rail in position and secure it with a screw at each end. Check for squareness and adjust as necessary, then add two more screws *(right)*. Repeat the procedure for the other leg and for the second pair of legs.

Leg

Rail

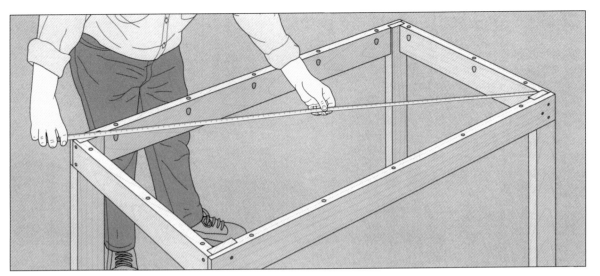

4 **Adding end rails.** To attach each end rail, drill clearance holes in each end; then, apply glue to the rabbets. With the help of an assistant to hold up the sides on a level surface, position one of the rails and screw it in place with one screw. Check to make sure that it is square, then add another screw.

Repeat the process for each corner. Check the table base for square by taking a measurement across each diagonal; they should be equal *(above)*. If not, place a clamp over the longer diagonal and tighten it slowly until the two distances are equal. Leave the clamp in place until the glue cures.

Preparing the Lattice Frame

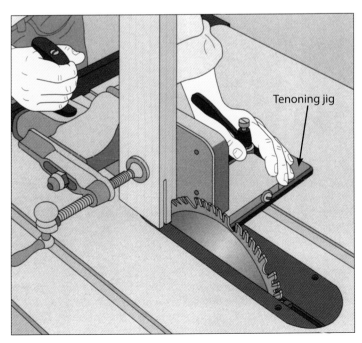

Tenoning jig

1 **Cutting tenon cheeks.** The corners of the lattice frame are joined with bridle joints for extra strength. The first step is to cut the tenon cheeks. If you are working with a table saw you will need a commercial tenoning jig or a shop-built device like the one like on page 89. To cut the cheeks, set the saw blade to its maximum height and mount the end of the frame in the tenoning jig. Adjust the jig so the blade meets the board at one third of the stock's thickness from the edge. Keep the kerf on the waste side. Turn on the saw and make a pass through the blade. Next, flip the board around and make the second cut *(left)*. Repeat for the opposite end then cut the cheeks in the other frame end.

2 Cutting shoulders. Once all the tenon cheeks have been cut, trim off the waste on the table saw to make the shoulders. Lay the frame rail on the table and adjust the blade height so it just touches the cheek. Attach an extension to the miter gauge. Hold the rail against the gauge and position the stock with the cutting mark for the shoulder in line with the blade. Clamp a stop block to the extension; this will speed up making repeat cuts. Then feed the stock into the blade *(right)*.

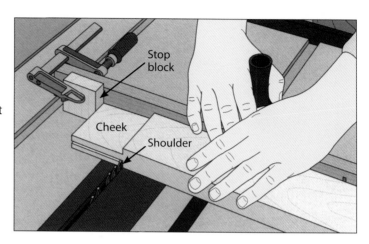

3 Cutting mortise cheeks. If your shop does not have a high ceiling you may not be able to cut the mortises in the stiles using the table saw and the tenoning jig. Instead, saw them by hand. With a rail tenon as a guide, mark the shoulder line and the cheeks of the mortise on the edges and end of each stile. Then mount the stock on your workbench at an angle as shown. This setup makes it easier to cut straight sides. With a back saw, cut down from the corner, keeping the blade on both lines *(above)*. Stop when the saw blade touches the shoulder line and the opposite corner. Cut its neighboring cheek, then turn the board over and cut the other diagonal kerfs. Finally, finish the cheeks by cutting straight down to the shoulder lines.

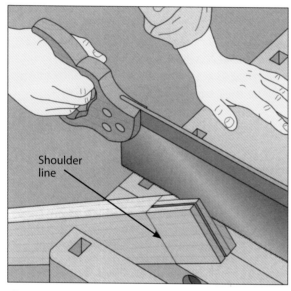

4 Chiseling mortise bottoms. Remove the waste between the mortise cheeks with a mallet and chisel. Mount the stile to your work bench as shown, clamping it firmly in place. Select a chisel the same width as the mortise, or as close as possible without being wider. To clean out the waste, place the chisel ⅛ inch in from the bottom of the mortise and tap it with a mallet so it sinks about ¼ inch. Set the chisel back toward the end of the board by about ¼ and tap towards the first cut to remove a small notch of waste. Continue in this manner until you reach about half-way. Turn the board over and remove the rest of the waste. Finally, pare straight down at the shoulder line *(above)*.

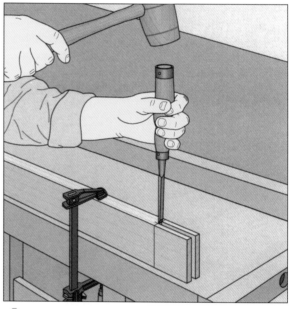

A Tenoning Jig for the Table Saw

You can use the jig shown at right to cut tenons on the table saw. Adapt the dimensions suggested in the illustration to customize the jig for your saw, if necessary.

Cut the jig fence and back from ¾-inch plywood and saw a 45° bevel at one end of each board; the pieces should be wider than the height of your saw's rip fence. Fasten two pieces together face to face to fashion the back, then use countersunk screws to attach the fence and back in an L shape. Make sure the fasteners will not be in the blade's path when you use the jig. Next, cut the brace from solid stock, bevel its ends, and attach it flush with the top edges of the fence and back, forming a triangle. Make the clamp by face gluing two pieces of ¾-inch plywood and cutting the assembly into the shape shown. Use a hanger bolt, washer, and wing nut to attach the clamp to the jig back, leaving a gap between the edge of the clamp and the fence equal to the thickness of the stock you will use. Offset the bolt so the clamp can pivot eccentrically. (You can drill additional holes in the jig back so you can shift the clamp to accommodate different stock thicknesses.) Next, cut the runner from solid wood. When attached to the jig fence, the runner will straddle the saw fence, eliminating any wobble. For some models, you will have to mill a groove down the length of the runner, as shown, to fit the rip fence. Finally, cut a piece of clear plastic as a blade guard and screw it to the jig back flush with its front face.

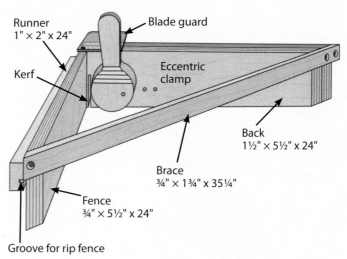

Runner
1" × 2" x 24"

Blade guard

Kerf

Eccentric clamp

Back
1½" × 5½" x 24"

Brace
¾" × 1¾" x 35¼"

Fence
¾" × 5½" x 24"

Groove for rip fence

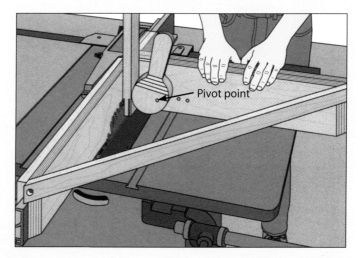

Pivot point

To use the jig, set it on the saw table in front of the blade with the runner and fence straddling the rip fence. Clamp the workpiece in the jig and position the rip fence to align the cutting mark on the workpiece with the blade. Feed the jig into the cutting edge. (Your first use of the jig will produce a kerf in the back.) Flip the workpiece around and repeat to cut the other cheek *(above)*. Remove the jig to cut the shoulders.

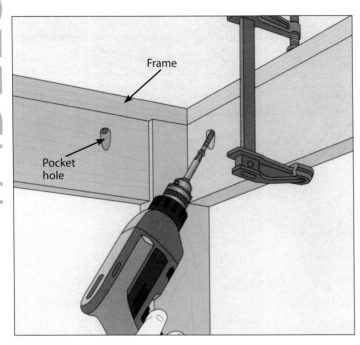

Frame

Pocket hole

5 **Attaching the frame.** Once you have cut the bridle joints, dry assemble the frame and set it on the table base to ensure that it fits properly. There should be a ¾ inch ledge all around the inside edge of the frame, which will support the lattice grid. Disassemble the frame and spread some glue on the tenons. Reassemble the frame, check for squareness, and clamp each joint with a pair of clamps. Then round over the outside edges of the frame. To secure the frame in position, set it on the rails and arrange it to create an even ¾ inch ledge. Hold the frame in place with a clamp in each corner and secure it with a screw in each pocket hole *(left)*.

Assembling the Lattice Grid

1 **Dadoing the cross strips.** The strips that make up the lattice grid are joined with half-lap joints—more than 300 in total. Position the dadoes with a simple indexing jig. Mount a ¾-inch-wide dado head on your table saw and adjust the blade height to half the width of the stock. Fix the jig to a miter gauge extension to leave 1½ inch space between dadoes. Start with stock one inch longer then the nominal lengths given in the cutting list. To cut the first dado in each piece hold it on edge against the miter gauge with one end butted against the key. Make a pass through the cutters, then move the board along the gauge, fitting the new dado over the key, and make another pass. Continue in this manner until you have cut dadoes in all the short and long strips.

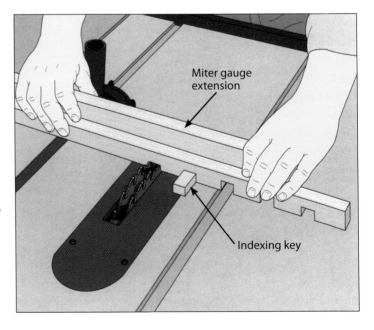

Miter gauge extension

Indexing key

2 Sizing the strips. Both the long and short strips must be trimmed to fit inside the frame. Lay a short strip across the frame and adjust it until the distance between the last dado and the frame is the same on both ends. Make a mark on the strip *(right)*. To trim the strip to this mark install a regular blade in your table saw. Next, reposition the miter gauge extension so that when the last dado is fitted over the key, the trimming mark is lined up with the blade. Trim the ends of this strip, then trim both ends of all the short strips the same way. Repeat this procedure to trim the long strips.

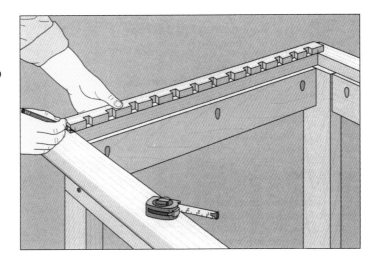

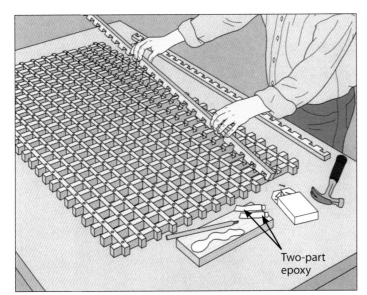

Two-part epoxy

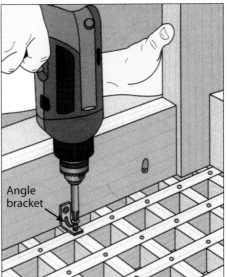

Angle bracket

3 Assembling the grid. Assemble the grid, then install it as one unit in the frame. Lay out all the short strips—dadoed edges up—on a large work surface. Space them out by installing a long strip at each end. Next, install the rest of the long strips, applying glue first and working the dadoes together gently *(above)*. Anchor each joint with a 1-inch galvanized common nail. Once all the long strips are in place, remove the outside long strips and reinstall them with glue and nail them in place.

4 Installing the grid. Pop the grid in place, then turn the table upside down. Install angle brackets to secure the lattice in position. To make sure the grid rests flat, screw each bracket to the rails with a ⅛ inch space between it and the lattice strip. After attaching a bracket to its rail, secure it to the corresponding lattice *(above)*. The gap will cause the bracket to be cinched down on the lattice, holding it tightly.

Folding Picnic Table and Bench

This picnic table is great for spontaneous afternoons in the country. It folds down flat to fit into most car trunks or hatchbacks. The key to its portability is the U-shaped leg assemblies, which nest inside each other. To acccomplish this, make the outer leg assembly first, then cut the inner one to fit inside it. This arrangement means, however, that one leg rail is short, and must rest on a block to provide the proper table height. The rail is held to the block with a butterfly catch.

The leg ends are marked and trimmed after the table is assembled, an easy way to get exactly the right angle and length.

The perfect complement to the picnic table is the keyed tenon bench. Also known as a joynt stool, it is an adaptation of an old English design that features an interesting construction technique. The legs are made in halves, then joined with dowel joints to ensure symmetry, while the notches automatically form the through mortises to hold the stretchers in place.

Cutting List	Qty	T	W	L
Picnic table				
Outer legs	2	1½"	3½"	36"*
Inner legs	2	1½"	3½"	36"*
Hinge rail	1	1½"	3½"	36"
Catch rail	1	1½"	3½"	29"
Cross rail	1	1½"	3½"	29"
Top rails	2	1¼"	4"	27"
Top stiles	2	1¼"	4"	44"
Butterfly catch support block	1	1¾"	4¾"	19¾"
Top slats	7	1¼"	4"	48"
Hinge supports	2	1¼"	3"	6"
Bench				
Leg halves	4	1¼"	5½"	16"
Upper stretcher	1	1¼"	3"	28½"
Lower stretcher	1	1¼"	3"	34"
Cleats	4	1¼"	1¼"	4⅞"
Seat slats	3	1¼"	4¾"	36"
Tusks	2	½"	1"	4" *Not final length

Anatomy of a Bench

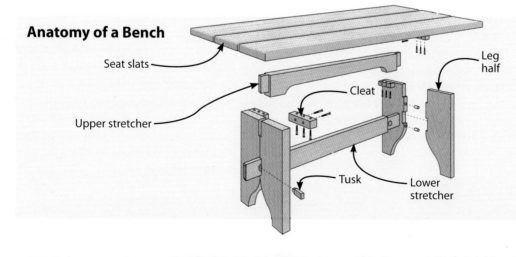

Seat slats

Upper stretcher

Cleat

Leg half

Tusk

Lower stretcher

Anatomy of a Picnic Table

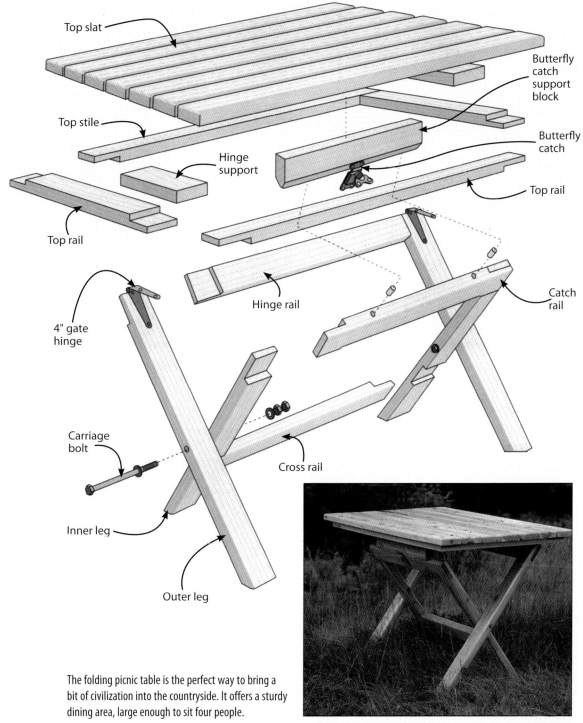

Top slat

Butterfly catch support block

Top stile

Hinge support

Butterfly catch

Top rail

Top rail

Catch rail

Hinge rail

4" gate hinge

Carriage bolt

Cross rail

Inner leg

Outer leg

The folding picnic table is the perfect way to bring a bit of civilization into the countryside. It offers a sturdy dining area, large enough to sit four people.

Folding Picnic Table

The picnic table's leg assemblies nest inside each other allowing it to fold as flat as possible.

Assembling the Top

Attaching frame. Cut the top slats to size according to the cutting list and round over their top edges and the ends. The top slats are secured to a rectangular frame which also holds the leg assemblies. Cut the frame's stiles and rails to size, then cut rabbets in their ends for the half-lap joints *(page 39)*. Glue the frame together and fasten it with screws. Check for squareness. To assemble the top, lay out the top slats on a work surface separated by ¼ inch spacers. Hold them together with a bar clamp at each end. Center the frame on the top, checking with a measuring tape that the borders along the sides and the ends are even. Secure the frame with a pair of screws into each slat *(right)*. Do not use any glue here, so it will be a simple matter to replace broken or rotten slats in the future.

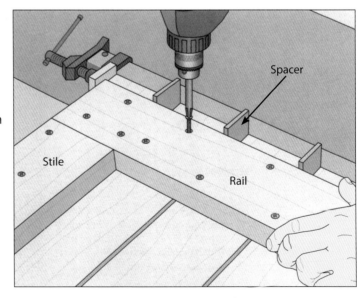

Spacer

Stile

Rail

Making Leg Assemblies

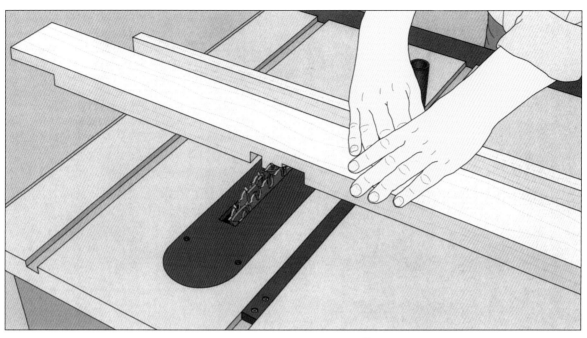

1 Preparing leg pieces. Cut the legs and adjoining rails to size; then, cut the rabbets for the half-laps in the legs and the rails. Next, mark out a 3½ inch dado for the cross rail on the inner legs, starting 21 inches fron the top. To make the dadoes, make two passes, cutting out the extremes of the dado, then remove the rest of the waste *(above)*.

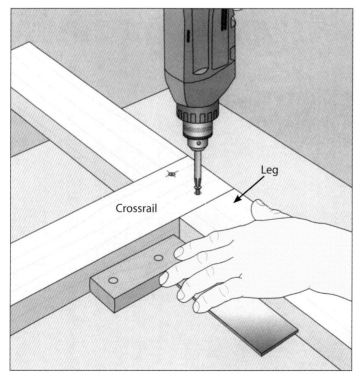

Leg

Crossrail

2 Fastening legs and rails. Starting with the outer leg assembly, lay the legs on a work surface and apply glue to the rabbets. To attach each rail, place it in position on the legs and secure it with one screw at each end. Check that it is perfectly square, then add the second screw. Before assembling the inner legs and rails, double check that the rails will fit inside the outer assembly, otherwise the legs will not fold properly. If necessary, trim the rails and adjust their rabbets to compensate. Assemble the inner legs as above, then add the crossrail *(left)*.

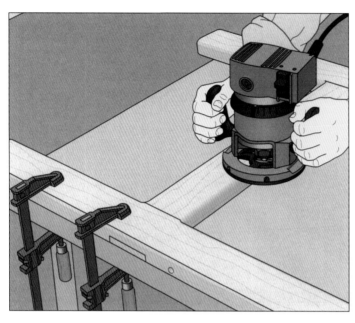

3 **Rounding over the legs and rails.** Round over the legs and rails after they have been assembled. Set the depth of cut to remove the waste in two passes. Clamp the assembly to a work surface. Turn on the router and ease the bit into the wood until the bearing touches, then work the router around the workpiece, making sure that you move against the bit's direction of rotation *(left)*. Reposition the clamps as necessary. Then round over the other leg assembly.

4 **Fitting carriage bolts.** Set the two leg assemblies on a work surface as shown, with the smaller one nested inside the larger one, then clamp them to the table. Mark the holes for the bolts on both assemblies, 18 inches from the top of the hinge rail. Fit a drill with a 5/16-inch bit, then bore the hole, keeping the bit perfectly perpendicular to the edge. It helps to have an assistant sight the bit to keep it level. Drill as deep as you can, then finish from the other side. Tap the carriage bolts through the legs with a hammer, then slide on a washer. Hand tighten two nuts, then fit a wrench on both nuts and hold the inner one in place while tightening the outer one against it *(right)*.

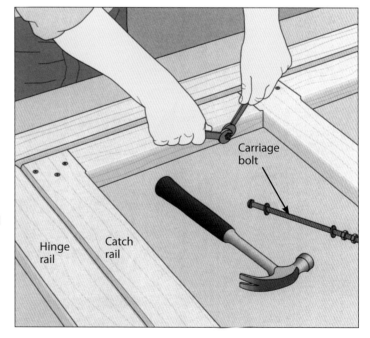

Carriage bolt

Hinge rail

Catch rail

Installing Legs

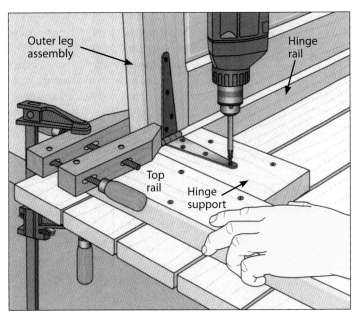

Outer leg assembly

Hinge rail

Top rail

Hinge support

1 **Attaching the hinges.** Screw the hinge support to the underside of the table-top where the rails and stiles meet. Then position the outer leg assembly on the top stile and hold it upright with a handscrew *(left)*. Arrange the assembly so the hinge will be 3⅝ inches from the outside edge of the stile. Then screw the hinge to the leg before attaching it to the tabletop.

2 **Adding the butterfly catch support block.** Cut the block to size according to the cutting list, ripping one edge at 30 degrees, leaving a 4-inch-high outside face. Saw the opposite face of the block at 60 degrees. Apply glue to the table where the block will touch it and clamp the block securely. Drill a pilot hole every 4 inches, then screw the block in place *(below)*.

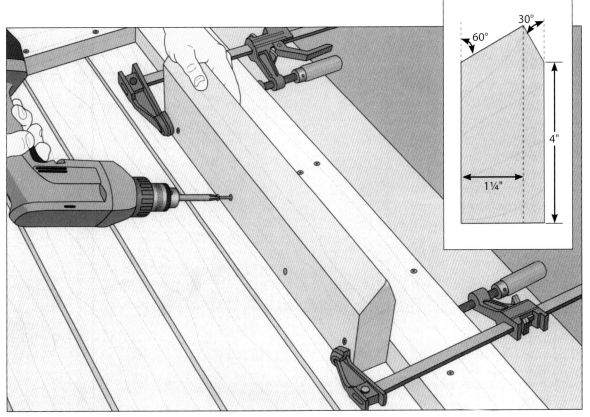

30°

60°

4"

1¼"

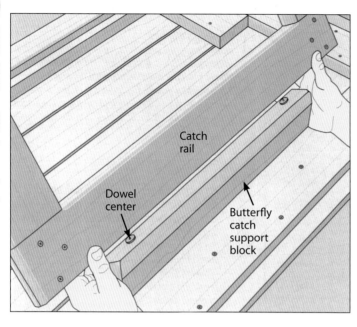

Catch rail

Dowel center

Butterfly catch support block

3 **Installing the dowels.** To bolster the union between the butterfly catch support block and the edge of the catch rail, install a pair of ½-inch dowels. To fit the dowels, first drill two ½-inch holes in the block, perpendicular to the angled face, to a depth of about ¾ inch. Place dowel centers in the holes and bring the catch rail into position *(left)*. Push down on the rail to mark the dowel holes. Drill 1-inch-deep holes in the rail. Spread glue inside the block holes and tap two 1½ inch long dowels into place. Then screw the butterfly catch to the rail and support block. The photograph on page 81 shows the catch in operation.

Fitting Legs

1 **Marking the legs.** The position of the legs makes it difficult to mark their length so they will sit perfectly level with the help of only a tape measure. One trick is to trim a piece of scrap plywood to a width of 28 inches and use that as a guide. To mark the inner legs, clamp a carpenter's square to the guide to hold it upright and set it against the leg as shown. Hold a try square against the board and mark the cutoff length and angle *(right)*. To mark the outer legs, it is possible to simply hold the marking board against the leg edge and trace the line. With the try square, run the lines around all four sides of each leg.

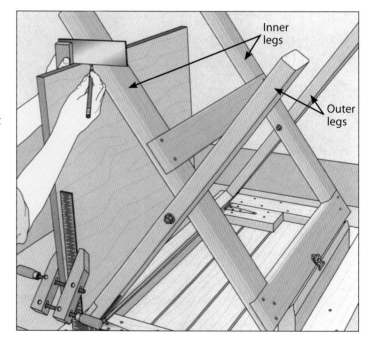

Inner legs

Outer legs

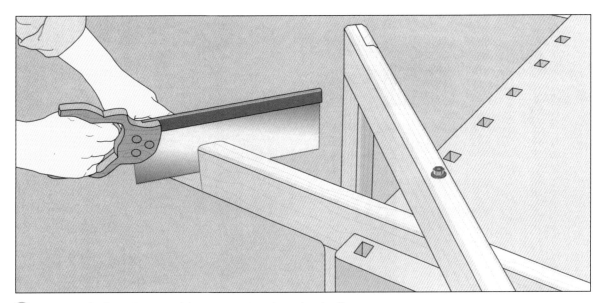

2 Trimming the legs. To trim each leg, mount it in a vise and cut it off with a backsaw, keeping the saw both on the top edge line and the line on the closest face. Once the kerf extends across the top edge, continue cutting straight down *(above)*. Keep checking both lines to make sure the saw does not wander.

Shop Tip

Replaceable feet

One of the problems of the legs of outdoor furniture is that the end grain naturally acts as a wick to draw moisture into the leg, hastening the decaying process. A simple solution is to add ¼-inch-thick blocks, whose grain runs lengthwise. These will be slower to pick up moisture and can be easily replaced when they eventually do rot.

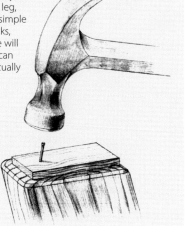

3 Rounding feet. Every time the table is moved, you risk catching an edge and splintering the bottom. To prevent this, round over the bottoms of the legs with a random orbit sander *(above)* or a sanding block.

Keyed Tenon Bench

The keyed tenon bench, also known as a joynt stool, is a handy seat that can be made in almost any length. It is the perfect complement to the picnic table but is useful all by itself.

Making the Legs

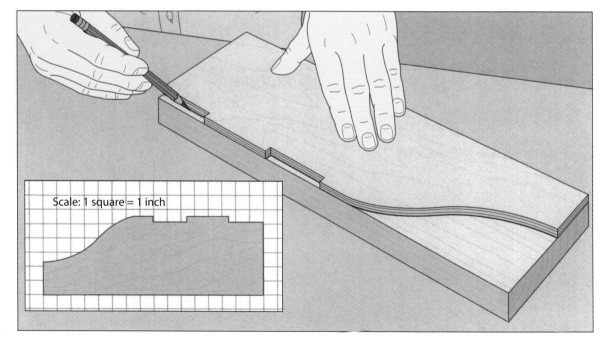

Scale: 1 square = 1 inch

1 Marking leg boards. The leg boards are made in halves, then glued together with dowel joints. To mark the leg board halves make a template, referring to the diagram in the inset. Prepare the legs according to the cutting list. Check that the notched edges are perfectly straight so they will form a tight glue joint. Set the template on the leg stock and mark out the curve and the notches.

2 **Cutting the leg boards.** Cut out the legs on the band saw. Start with the curve, simply cutting on or just outside the marked line. To cut out the notches, first make a short cross-grain cut to define the mortise end. Next make a sweeping cut towards, then along, the mortise side line until you reach the other crossgrain mark. Cut this section free *(right)*. Finally reorient the board and remove the rest of the waste. Sand off any machining marks from the curve.

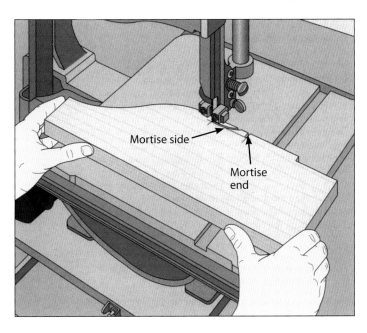

Mortise side

Mortise end

TABLES · *Keyed Tenon Bench*

3 **Joining leg halves.** Join the leg halves with dowel joints. To prepare the legs for the dowels, drill two ½ inch diameter holes, 1 inch deep into one half. Mark the opposite legs with dowel centers *(see page 98)*. Position the tops of the legs against a straight edge such as a rip fence to make sure the notches will line up. Spread some glue inside the holes and along the straight edges of the legs. Push the two halves together *(left)* and clamp the leg with a bar clamp opposite each of the two glued edges (not opposite the notches).

Assembling the Bench

1 Cutting tenons in the stretchers. Prepare the stretchers referring to the cutting list, then rabbet their ends to make the tenons. The top stretcher tenon should be 1¼ inches long to end flush with the legs, while the lower one must be 4 inches long to allow it to hold a tusk pin. To cut the rabbets, install a dado cutting assembly in your table saw and attach a miter gauge extension. Adjust the cutting height to about ¼ inch and make a cut in both sides of a piece of scrap stock and test the fit in the open mortise. Fine tune the height until the test tenon fits snugly. Set the rip fence to make a 1¼-inch-long tenon. To cut the tenon, hold the stock against the miter gauge extension with an end butted against the fence. Pass the wood over the cutters, then remove the rest of the waste by moving the workpiece away from the fence in successive passes. Repeat for the other side and the opposite end. Next, raise the cutters to ½ inch, hold the stretcher on its lower edge, and cut a notch to allow the stretcher to fit flush with the top of the legs. Reset the fence to make a 4-inch-long tenon and make the cut in the lower stretcher *(right)*. Then saw a ¼-inch notch in the top and bottom edges to allow the piece to fit into the mortise.

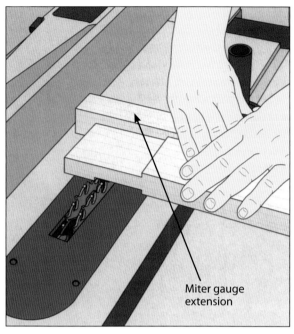

Miter gauge extension

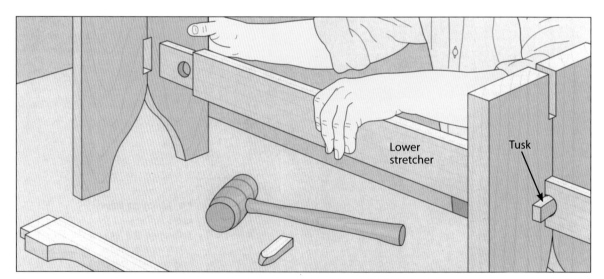

Lower stretcher

Tusk

2 Installing the stretchers. Install the lower stretcher first. To prepare the tenon for the tusk pin, bore a 1-inch-diameter hole centered 2¼ inches from the tenon end. Then insert the stretcher in the leg *(above)*. Do not press down on the outside edges of the legs to force them over the tenon; this is liable to split them. Instead, knock the leg on both sides of the tenons with the the heel of your hand. When the stretcher is in place, the tenon should reveal a ½-inch semicircle to hold the tusk. Whittle and sand the tusk stock so it fits tightly in the opening. Make it slightly wedge-shaped so it tightens the joint the further it is inserted. Tap the tusk in place with a mallet. Finally, apply glue to the upper mortise and slide the top stretcher in place.

3 **Attaching the seat-support cleats.** To avoid having screw holes in the top of the seat, secure the slats to the legs with cleats. Trim the cleats so they fit on either side of the top stretcher. Drill the pilot holes for attaching the slats off center to make it easier to tighten the screws into the seat without knocking your hands against the legs. Apply glue to the cleats, then secure them to the legs with screws so the strips are flush with the top of the legs *(right)*.

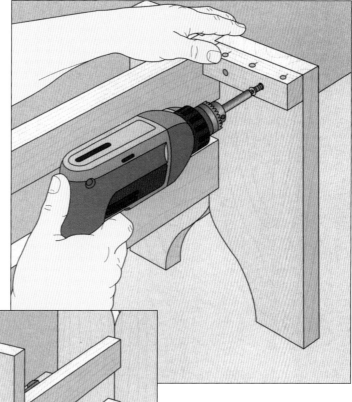

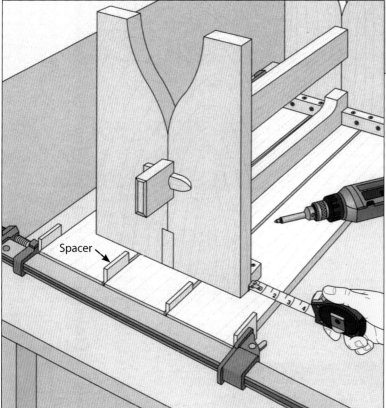

4 **Securing the slats.** Round over the top edges of the slats, then lay them out on a work surface, separated by ¼-inch spacers. Make sure the ends are all even, and tighten a bar clamp across each end to hold the slats in place. Center the bench base on the slats and secure it with screws *(left)*.

Spacer

TABLES | *Keyed Tenon Bench*

SWINGS AND GLIDERS

Rocking motions are comforting to people of all ages. Pleasant and relaxing, a swing or a gliding settee provides an ideal accessory to a porch or garden. The two projects shown in this chapter also offer interesting mechanical challenges to a furniture maker. These pieces must be strong and lightweight. They must also stand up to a stress that furniture rarely has to endure—constant movement.

There are several ways to achieve a rocking motion. The simplest solution is to suspend the seat with rope or chain. This requires a sturdy branch or structural member to support the swing. The glider support uses a different system to impart a swinging motion. Four lengths of metal strap support the bench within a low frame. Other methods use commercially available roller bearings.

It is important to buy hardware that is as corrosion-resistant as possible, especially for these pieces of furniture that are difficult to cart indoors for the winter. Stainless steel straps and screws, although more expensive than their regular steel counterparts, are strong and will not rust. Brass screws are not so strong, but offer a decorative option that is also corrosion-resistant. If you use brass, drive in a steel screw first to tap the hole, then remove it and install the brass screw, taking care not to overtighten or you will risk breaking off the head.

The porch swing is shown beginning on page 106, while the glider frame section starts on page 114. The bench that fits this particular frame is shown in the Benches chapter starting on page 66.

The glider bench shown above swings on two metal straps mounted on each side of a support frame. The rub rail at the bottom acts as a spacer, preventing the bench from bumping against the frame as the glider rocks back and forth.

Although many people choose to hang a swing on a porch, you can also suspend yours from a tree branch, as shown at left, providing a shady spot for visitors to linger and relax.

Porch Swing

The back seat rail is beveled to a 15° to 25° angle, so as to provide a comfortable angle for the seat back. The back is screwed and glued onto the rail, the same method used to join most of the frame. The arms, which provide additional support for the back, are the exception to the glue-and-screw method. They are fastened together by cross dowels. These are strong joints, but must be carefully installed to work properly.

Note that the stiles of the seat back are located in front of the rails so that the joint line is vertical, promoting good water drainage for a long-lived joint.

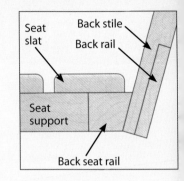

Cross dowels are commonly used in knockdown furniture, but their strength and durability make them ideal for outdoor furniture that is not designed to be taken apart. A cross-dowel connector is used to join an arm to an arm post in the chair shown above, providing a much stronger connection than screws could, and saving the task of fashioning a more elaborate joint.

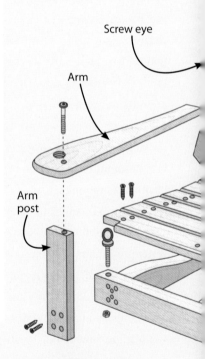

Cutting List

Item	Qty	Th	W	L
Back slats	13	½"	2"	24¼"
Seat slats	6	¾"	3³⁄₁₆"	55½"
Back rails	2	1⅛"	4¾"	55"
Back stiles	2	1⅛"	4¾"	28"
Front seat rail	1	2"	3½"	60"
Back seat rail	1	1¾"	2"	60"
Rail cover	1	¼"	4¾"	45½"
Seat supports	4	1¾"	3½"	15¾"
Arms	2	¾"	5¾"	24"
Arm posts	2	¾"	2⅞"	11½"

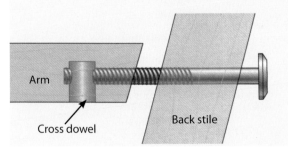

Anatomy of a Porch Swing

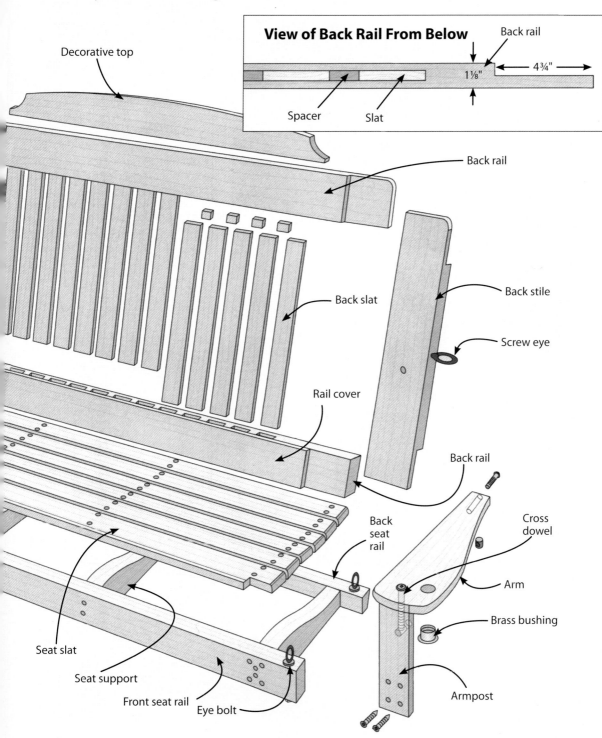

View of Back Rail From Below

Back rail

Spacer

Slat

$1\frac{1}{8}$"

$4\frac{3}{4}$"

Decorative top

Back rail

Back stile

Back slat

Screw eye

Rail cover

Back rail

Back seat rail

Cross dowel

Arm

Brass bushing

Seat slat

Seat support

Front seat rail

Eye bolt

Armpost

Preparing the Back Rails

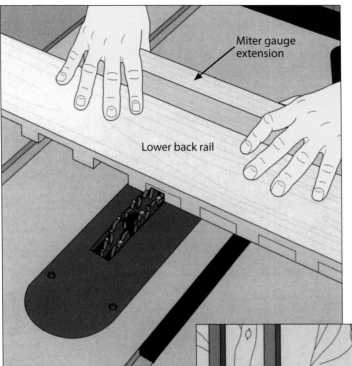

Miter gauge extension

Lower back rail

1 **Sawing dadoes in the lower back rail.** To prepare the rail for the slats, you will need to cut 2-inch-wide, ½-inch-deep dadoes in the stock. First, fit your table saw with a dado head and adjust it to maximum width, then attach an extension board to the miter gauge. Check the cutting height by making a test cut on scrap stock and adjust the blades until the cut is the same depth as the thickness of your slats. Mark the dado outlines on the leading edge of the workpiece, beginning 8½ inches from each end and spacing the dadoes 1 inch apart. For each dado, saw the outside edges, then cut away the waste in the center *(left)*. **(Caution: Blade guard removed for clarity.)**

2 **Attaching the rail cover.** Cut the rail cover to size, then spread glue on the dadoed face of the rail and the rail cover. Position the two pieces together and tack the cover in place with brads, making sure not to nail any brads within 5 inches of either end of the nail. Next, clamp the assembly, making sure you apply pressure to every gluing surface *(right)*.

Rail cover

Lower back rail

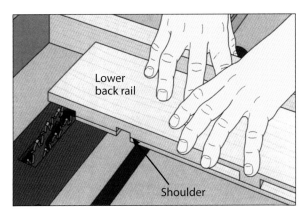

3 Cutting corner half-laps. The back assembly is composed of stiles joined to the two rails with half-laps. To cut the joint, use the same setup you made for sawing dadoes in the lower back rail. This time mark out the half-laps at the end of each rail and stile. The joint should be as wide as the stile stock. Butt the stock against the miter gauge extension, and line up the blades to cut the shoulder of the half-lap first. Then saw away the remaining waste with multiple passes *(above)*. Repeat the procedure to cut the joint at the other end of the stock and in the remaining rail and stiles.

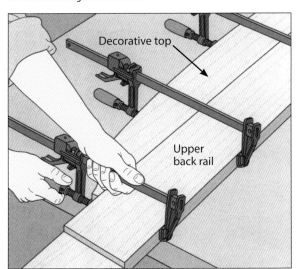

4 Decorating the top rail. Referring to the anatomy illustration on page 107, trace the shape of the decorative top on the stock and cut it to shape with a band saw. Then attach it to the upper back rail with glue and clamp the two pieces together *(above)*.

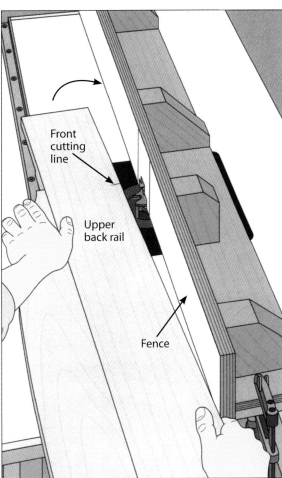

5 Grooving the top rail. You need to rout a groove in the upper back rail to hold the back slats. Fit a ½-inch three-wing slotting cutter in a router, then mount the tool in a table. Mark the points on the face of the stock where the cut should start and end. Also mark the points on the fence where the bit starts and stops cutting. Adjust the height to center the groove in the edge of the rail. Turn on the router and pivot the rail into the cutter, aligning the front cutting line on the workpiece with the bit cutting mark on the fence farthest from you *(above)*. Push the rail along the fence until the back cutting line aligns with the bit cutting mark closest to you, then pivot the trailing edge of the workpiece away from the cutter, steadying the board against the table and fence by hooking your left hand around the front edge of the table. Use a chisel to square the ends of the groove, if necessary.

Assembling the Back

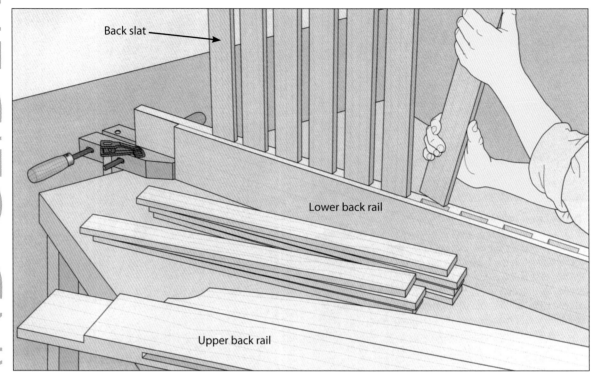

Back slat

Lower back rail

Upper back rail

1 Installing the slats. Clamp the lower rail so it stands right-side up on your work surface. Fit a slat into each notch *(above)* and tap the slats until the ends are flush with the bottom of the rail. Drive a finishing nail into each slat through the back of the rail to secure the piece in place, then fit the upper back rail onto the slats.

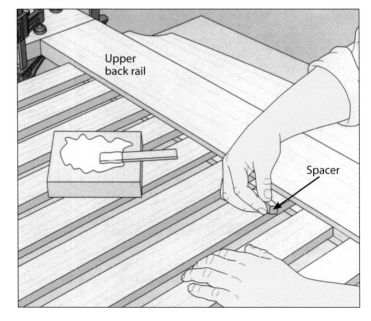

Upper back rail

Spacer

2 Gluing up the back assembly. Lay the partially assembled seat back on your work surface. Apply adhesive to the corner lap joints of the rails and stiles and clamp the assembly together. Then glue spacers in the groove between the slats in the upper back rail *(right)*.

Assembling the Seat

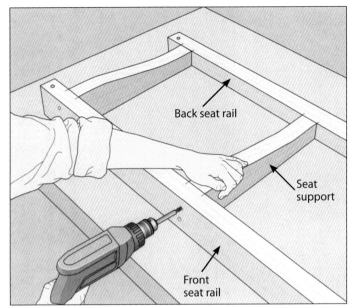

Back seat rail

Seat support

Front seat rail

1 **Assembling the frame.** Cut a 15° to 20° bevel on the rear face of the back seat rail, using a table saw with the blade tilted to the appropriate angle. Then prepare four seat supports, copying their shape from the anatomy *(page 107)*. Cut the pieces on a band saw, using the first support as a template for the others. Smooth the edges on a spindle sander. Glue and screw the frame together, locating the outside supports 2 inches from the ends of the rails *(above)*.

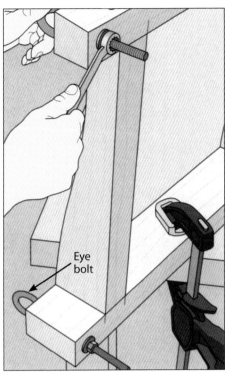

Eye bolt

2 **Attaching the eye bolts.** Drill a hole through the protruding end of each seat rail just large enough to accommodate a stainless-steel eye bolt. Slip the eye bolt in place, add a washer and nut, and tighten the bolt firmly in place *(above)*. Trim the excess bolt, if necessary.

3 **Attaching the back to the seat frame.** Clamp the seat frame beveled-edge up on a work surface. Spread glue on the edge and on the front face of the lower rail of the seat back. Clamp the back to the seat frame, then drill pilot holes and screw the two assemblies together *(right)*.

Installing the Arms and Seat Slats

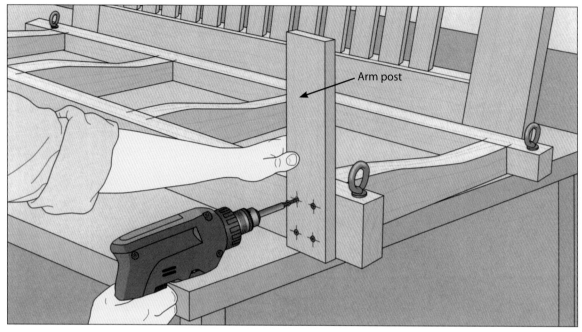

Arm post

1 Attaching the arm posts. Position the arm post 2 inches from the end of the front seat rail flush with the bottom of the rail. Drill 4 pilot holes, then glue the arm post in place and secure it with screws *(above)*. Repeat the procedure for the second arm post.

2 Attaching the arm with cross dowels. Cut out the arms on a band saw, referring to the anatomy for their shape. There is both a right and left arm, so be sure not to mix them up. Round over the edges of the arms with a router fitted with a round-over bit. Then use a bevel gauge to transfer the angle of the chair back to the back edge of the arm and make the cut on your table saw. This will allow the arm, which is horizontal, to fit flush against the chair back. Then drill a hole the same diameter as the cross-dowel bolt through the arm into the arm post. Make sure you drill straight. Next, bore a hole into the arm post for the cross-dowel connector about 2 inches from the top of the post, intercepting the bolt hole at 90°. Insert the connector in its hole, then slide the bolt into position and tighten it with a hex wrench *(right)*. Install cross dowels in the same fashion to connect the back of the seat to the arm. Repeat the procedure to attach the second arm.

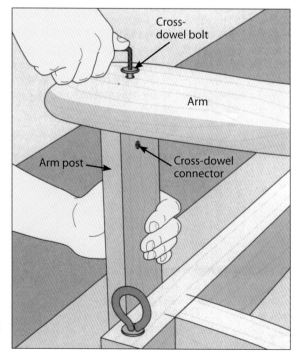

Cross-dowel bolt

Arm

Arm post

Cross-dowel connector

Assembling the Chair

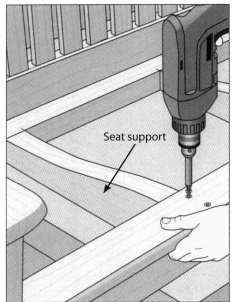

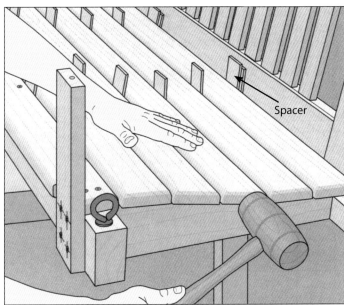

1 Adding the seat slats. Round over the front and back edges of the slats. Then install the front seat slat, notching it to fit around the arm posts. The front edge of the slat should be flush with the front of the arm post; the ends of the slats should project beyond the edge of the end seat supports by ½ inch.

Mark the position of the supports and drill pilot holes, then screw the slat in place *(above, left)*. To install the remaining slats, use spacers ⅛ to ¼ inch thick to set the distance between the pieces. Tap the ends of the slats until they are all aligned *(above, right)*. Then drill pilot holes and screw the slats in place.

2 Attaching the chains. Install a screw eye in each of the seat back stiles 2 inches above the arm. Then mark the point on each arm directly over the front eye bolt and drill a hole to accommodate a 1¾-inch-diameter brass bushing. Insert the bushing and fasten it in place. Attach a length of chain with an opening link to each of the eye bolts in the seat rails *(right)*. Thread the chain from the front eye bolts through the bushings; the chain from the rear eye bolts passes through the screw eyes in the back stiles. Join the chains on each side of the chair in pairs with opening chain links, giving you two points from which the chair can be hung.

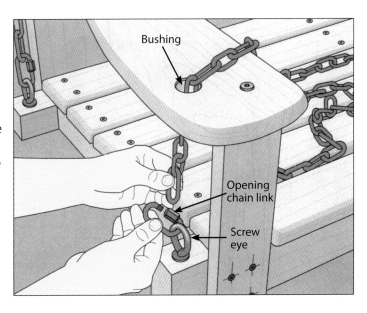

Glider Base

This versatile glider base can be adapted to fit different designs of benches. In this case, it has been constructed to support the bench shown on page 66. With simple changes, this design could easily add swinging motion to a chair, or a bench up to three persons wide.

The base consists of two side frames connected by two central beams that are separated by a spacer. The frames are made of rails and stiles joined with corner half-laps. The beams can be shortened or lengthened as necessary, depending on the size of the bench or chair, but remember that the longer the bench, the more its weight, and therefore the greater the stress on the glider base.

The bench swings on 18-inch metal straps. They should be angled slightly inward so the top ends are farther apart than the lower ends. This will tend to slow the glider down as it approaches the ends of its swing. It also reduces mechanical stresses on the bench and glider frame.

Cutting List

Length	Qty	Th	W	L
Side frame rails	4	1¾"	3½"	28"
Side frame stiles	4	1¾"	3½"	20"
Feet	2	1¾"	3½"	34"
Foot pads	4	1¾"	3½"	5¾"
Spacer blocks	2	1¼"	1¾"	3½"
Center beams	2	1¾"	3½"	50⅝"
Support straps	4	⅛"	1"	18"

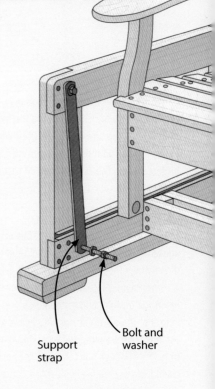

Support strap

Bolt and washer

The advantage of a glider base over a porch swing is that it is self-supporting and can be placed wherever you want—on a porch or in a garden—without requiring supporting beams or tree branches. The base features a metal rub rail at the bottom to prevent the bench from bumping against the base as it glides back and forth.

Anatomy of a Glider Base

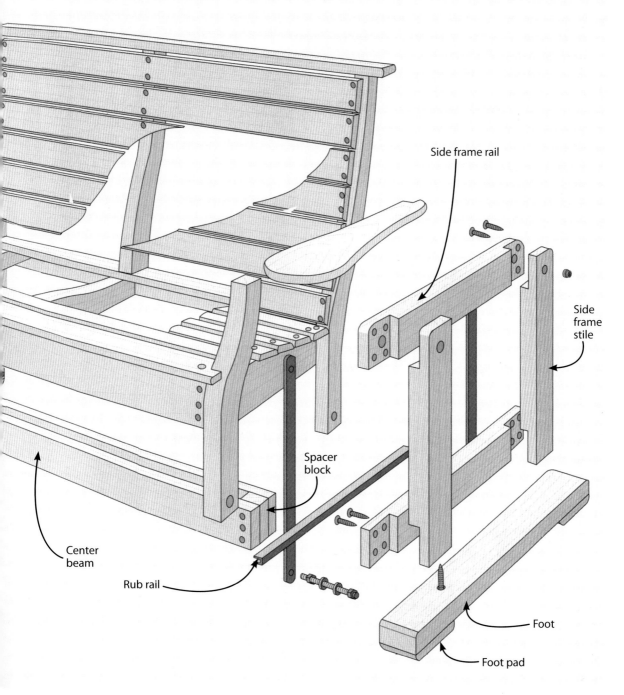

Side frame rail

Side frame stile

Center beam

Spacer block

Rub rail

Foot

Foot pad

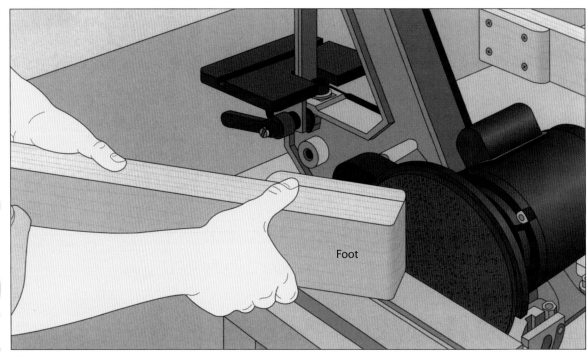

Foot

1 Making the feet. Round over the back edge of each foot pad on a disk sander. Glue and screw the pads in place, with the front edge flush with the front of the foot. Then round over the front edges of each pad and foot *(above)*.

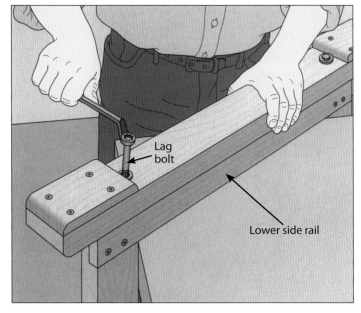

Lag bolt

Lower side rail

2 Assembling the sides. Cut half-lap joints in the side rails and stiles *(page 109)*. Assemble each joint with four screws and glue, then center the feet on the bottom of each side and drill a pilot hole 5¾ inches from each end into the lower side rails for a 3½-inch-long, ¼-inch-diameter lag bolt. Add a washer, then insert the bolt in the hole and tighten it with a wrench *(right)*.

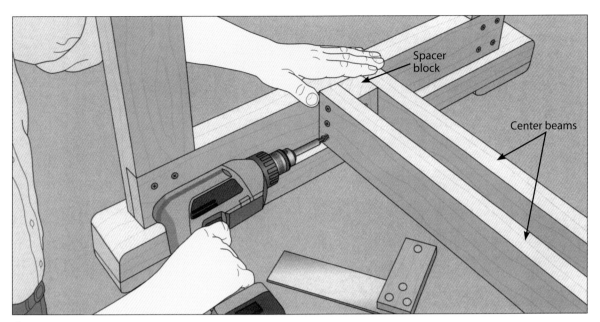

3 **Attaching the center beams to the sides.** Glue and screw a spacer block to the center of the inside face of each side rail. Then glue and screw the center beams on either side of each spacer block *(above)*, then attach the beams to the other spacer block, checking with a square on both lower side rails to make sure the assembly is perfectly square.

Installing the Gliders

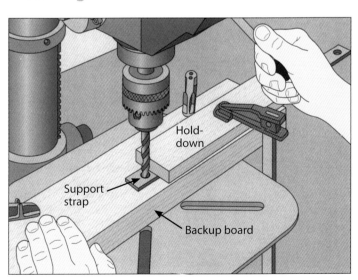

1 **Drilling the holes in the support straps.** Strike the strap with a center punch 1 inch from each end. This will dimple the surface, providing a starting point for your drill. Next, fit a ⅜-inch bit into your drill press. Clamp a piece of scrap wood to the machine table as a backup board, then position the strap with the mark you just made centered under the bit. Place a second piece of wood on top of the strap to prevent the drill bit from lifting the strap as the bit is retracted from the hole. Bore the hole *(left)*. Repeat at the other end and for the three other straps.

2 Drilling holes for the bushings. Mark out holes for ⅝-inch-diameter threaded bushings on the side rails and on the legs of the bench. This hardware will protect the wood from wear by the bolts that will secure the support straps to the frame and the piece of furniture. On the stand, locate each hole 1⅝ inches from the top edge and 2¼ inches from the outside edge. On the bench legs, the holes should be centered in the middle of the legs, 1 inch from the bottom. If you are adapting the stand to fit another piece of furniture, make sure that the ends of the metal straps are mounted a couple of inches closer together on the furniture than on the glider frame. This will improve the gliding motion. Drill holes for the bushings with a spade bit. Bore three-quarters of the way through each hole *(right)*, then complete the hole from the other side. Make sure the holes are square with the face of the frame.

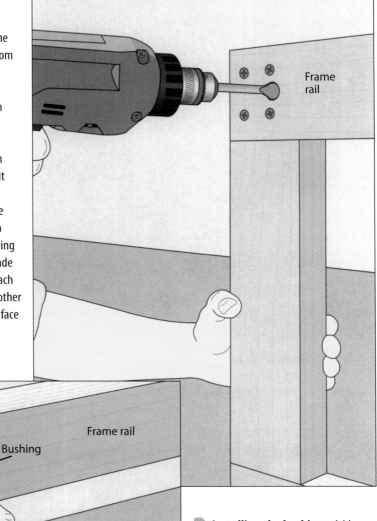

Frame rail

Bushing

Frame rail

3 Installing the bushings. Add threaded bushings by twisting them finger tight *(left)*, then finish tightening them with a screwdriver or a coin. If the bushing begins to enter the hole askew, remove it and enlarge the hole slightly with a rat-tail file. When it is installed, the bushing should rest slightly above the surface of the wood.

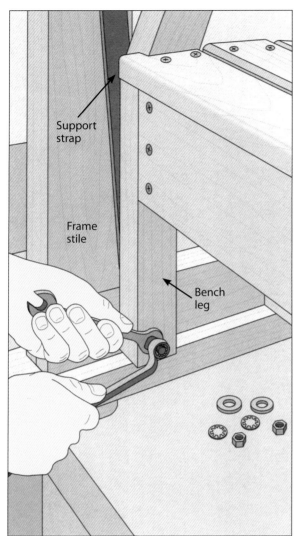

Support
strap

Frame
stile

Bench
leg

4 Bolting on the support straps. Slide a ¼-inch-diameter bolt through each of the support straps, slip on a washer, and fit the bolts through each of the bushings in the upper frame rail. Secure the bolts in place with a lock washer and two nuts, using a second wrench to hold one of the nuts in place while you tighten the other one. Next, position the bench between the sides of the frame, and repeat the bolting procedure. It will be easier to do this job with a helper to hold the bench in place while you slide the bolts through the bushings in the legs. Tighten the nuts *(left)*.

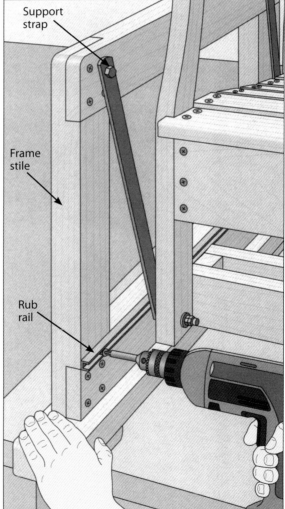

Support
strap

Frame
stile

Rub
rail

5 Adding the rub rail. The rub rail is a 28-inch-long piece of ½-inch aluminium C-stock. Drill a hole at each end, then place the rail between the support straps and the glider frame, with the lower edge of the rail flush with the upper edge of the bottom side rail. Screw the rub rail in place *(right)*, then attach the second rail on the opposite side of the glider frame.

GARDEN PROJECTS

The arbor, planter, and serving trolley presented in this chapter complement the furniture designs featured in previous chapters. The arbor creates a base for climbing plants and a decorative focal point for outdoor recreation or relaxation. Planters can be used to establish flowers or other plantings in any part of a garden. And with its capacity to transport both victuals and kitchen items like plates, dishes, and cutlery, the serving trolley is a welcome convenience for backyard entertaining.

The planter *(page 122)* is built from white cedar formed into staves. A ¾-inch piece of marine-grade plywood forms the bottom, and the staves are joined with spline-and-groove joints. A lip around the top edge protects the ends of the staves and adds a decorative element. For an eight-sided planter, the edges of the staves must be beveled at 22½°. The table-saw jig shown on page 123 will enable you to cut the bevels and taper the staves at the same time so they are wider at the top than at the bottom.

The serving trolley featured on page 128 is built around a frame joined with half-laps and reinforced by glue and screws. The slats on the bottom rest on cleats running along the inside faces of the lower side rails. The top consists of four rails that slip over the frame assembly, and are screwed to the top of the frame. The trolley rolls on two wheels of the type designed for gas barbecues. Indeed, the trolley could be used to replace the often flimsy metal bases provided with many barbecues.

The arbor is built from rough-sawn cedar *(page 133).* Left without a finish, the wood will turn an attractive silver hue as it weathers.

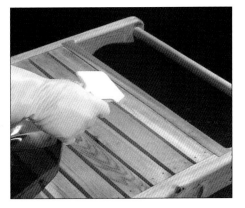

Tung oil is applied to the surface of a serving trolley. Using a squirt bottle as shown above is a quick and easy way to spread this finish. After being allowed to penetrate the wood for about 15 minutes, the excess oil is wiped from the surface with a rag.

Festooned with flowers, the rustic-style arbor shown at left frames a pathway from a backyard garden to a pond. The arbor is made from lattices of rough-sawn ¾-inch northern white cedar assembled with half-lap joinery.

Eight-Sided Planter

Anatomy of an Eight-Sided Planter

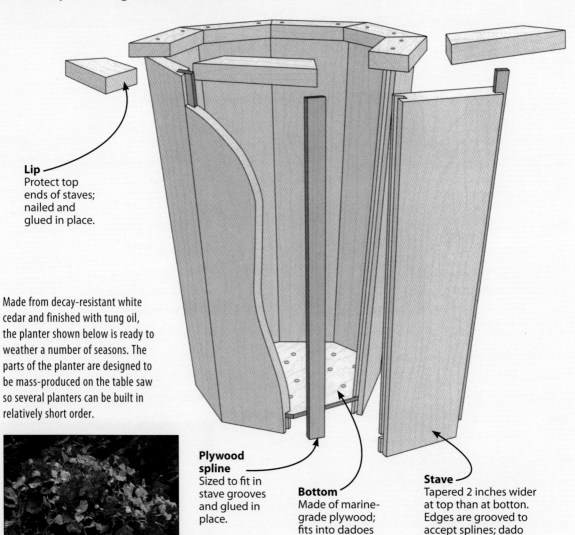

Lip
Protect top
ends of staves;
nailed and
glued in place.

Made from decay-resistant white
cedar and finished with tung oil,
the planter shown below is ready to
weather a number of seasons. The
parts of the planter are designed to
be mass-produced on the table saw
so several planters can be built in
relatively short order.

Plywood spline
Sized to fit in
stave grooves
and glued in
place.

Bottom
Made of marine-
grade plywood;
fits into dadoes
cut into staves.

Stave
Tapered 2 inches wider
at top than at bottom.
Edges are grooved to
accept splines; dado
cut across inside face
accommodates bottom.

Cutting List

Item	Qty	Th	W	L
Staves	8	¾"	6"	24"
Lips	8	¾"	2"	6½"
Bottom	1	¾"	18"	18"

Preparing the Staves

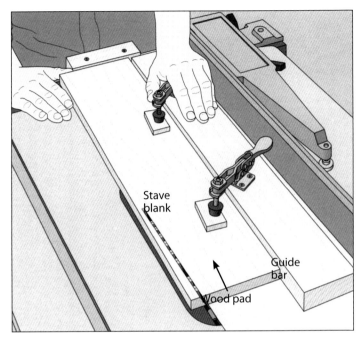

Stave blank

Guide bar

Wood pad

Jig base

1 Beveling one edge of the staves. With the shop-built tapering jig shown at left, you can bevel the edges of the staves and taper them in a single setup. For the jig, make the base from a piece of 12-inch-wide plywood, and the guide bar and stop block from solid stock. Start by angling the blade to 22½°, then use bar clamps to secure the stave blank to the base so the edge extends off the base by 1¼ inch at the leading end and ¼ inch at the trailing ends. Butt the guide bar and stop block against the stock, clamp them in place, and fix the pieces to the base. Screw toggle clamps to the guide bar and use them to secure the blank to the jig; protect the stock with wood pads. Remove the bar clamps. Next, butt the edge of the jig base against the blade and the rip fence against the opposite edge of the base. Start feeding the jig and workpiece with both hands, as shown, but move your right hand safely away about halfway through the cut. Finish the pass with your left hand, keeping the jig flush against the fence throughout. **(Caution: Blade guard removed for clarity.)** Bevel one edge of every stave the same way.

Shop Tip

Checking the saw blade bevel angle
To confirm that your table saw blade will cut a perfect 22½° angle, make test cuts at both ends of three wood scraps. Then place a carpenter's square on a flat surface and set one of the pieces on edge with its back face towards the corner of the square. Butt the other test pieces flush against the ends of the first one; their back faces should be flush against the arms of the square. If not, adjust the blade angle, recut the ends of the pieces, and recheck.

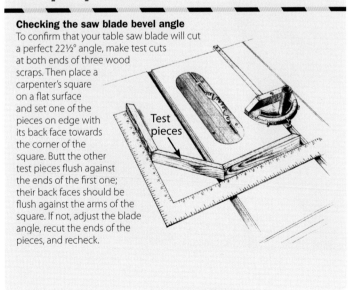

Test pieces

2 **Cutting the opposite edges.** To avoid having to adjust the blade angle when you bevel the opposite edge of each stave, clamp the blank to the base as in step 1, but with its narrow end at the leading end of the base. Make sure the narrow end of the blank extends off the base by 1¼ inch and the wide end by ¼ inch. Position the guide bar and stop block against the workpiece, and screw the pieces to the base from underneath *(left)*. Remove the bar clamps and bevel each stave.

Assembling the Planter

1 **Preparing the staves for the splines.** Fit your table saw with a dado head, adjust its width to the spline thickness—¼ inch—and set the cutting height to ⅜ inch. Center the edge of a stave over the blades, then butt the rip fence against one face of the stock and clamp a guide board to the saw table against the opposite face. Feed the stave into the head, keeping the outside face flush against the fence *(right)*. To determine the width of the plywood splines, secure two staves upright in handscrews, butt the pieces edge to edge, and measure the combined depth of their grooves *(inset)*. Cut the splines the same length as the staves, ripping them as wide as your measurement, less ⅛ inch.

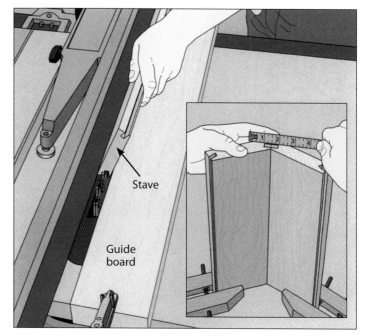

Stave

Guide
board

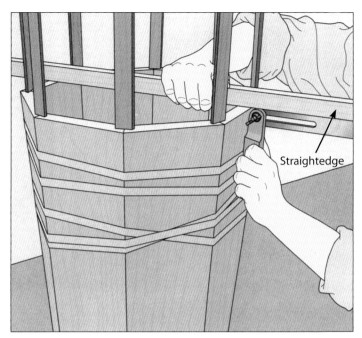

Straightedge

2 **Trimming the ends of the staves.** Once all the spline grooves have been cut, dry-fit the staves together with the splines. Use surgical tubing to hold the assembly together. To level the staves at the top and bottom, both ends of each piece will have to be beveled. To determine the bevel angle, hold a board as a straightedge across the top of the assembly and use a sliding bevel to measure the angle between the outside face of a stave and the straightedge *(left)*. Tilt your table saw blade to the measured angle and clamp an extension board to the miter gauge. Align the cutting mark at one end of the stave with the blade, then butt a stop block against the end of the stock and clamp it to the extension. Angle the miter gauge so the ends will be cut straight across. Then, holding the workpiece flush against the extension and stop block, bevel the end of each stave *(below)*. Use the same setup to bevel the opposite ends of the staves.

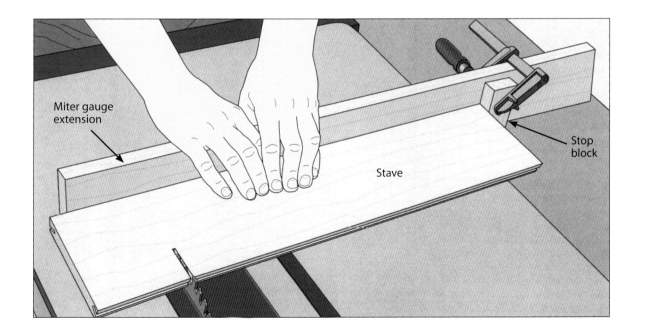

Miter gauge extension

Stop block

Stave

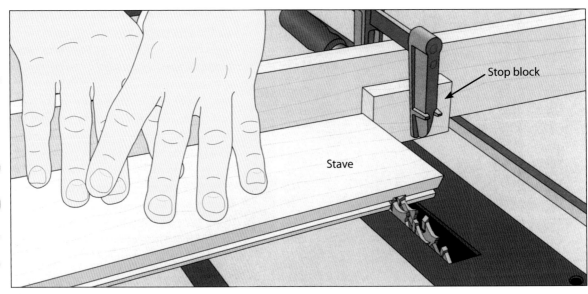

Stop block

Stave

3 Preparing the staves for the bottom. Cut dadoes across the inside faces of the staves for the bottom with a similar setup you used for crosscutting the staves. Adjust the width of the dado head to ¾ inch and tilt the blades to the same angle you measured in step 2. Set the cutting height to ⅜ inch. Clamp the stop block to the miter gauge extension to locate the dado ¾ inch from the bottom of the staves. Angle the miter gauge as you did in the previous step to compensate for the tapered sides of the staves. Hold the workpiece flush against the extension and the stop block as you feed it across the saw table *(above)*.

4 Cutting the bottom of the planter. Dry-fit the staves and splines together *(page 125)*. Center the assembly on a piece of ¾-inch marine-grade plywood and outline the outside of the planter on the workpiece. Then mark a second outline within the first, offset from it by ½ inch to compensate for the dadoes in the staves. Use the second outline as your cutting pattern as you saw out the bottom on your band saw *(right)*. Once the bottom is cut out, drill a few drainage holes through it.

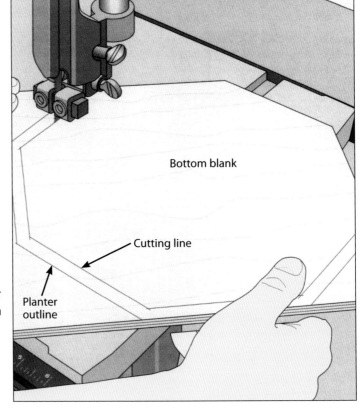

Bottom blank

Cutting line

Planter outline

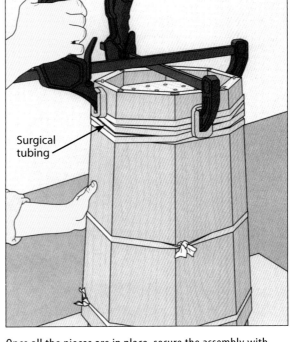

Surgical tubing

5 **Assembling the planter.** Test-fit all the pieces together, making sure the splines fit snugly in their grooves and the bottom fits into its dadoes. Use a chisel to fine-tune any ill-fitting joints. Spread glue in the spline grooves, then fit the staves around the bottom, slipping the splines in place as you go *(above, left)*. Push the splines down until their ends are flush with the bottom piece.

Once all the pieces are in place, secure the assembly with two lengths of surgical tubing, bicycle inner tube, or band clamps wrapped around the staves—one near the top and one near the bottom. Also install two bar clamps at each end of the planter on opposite sides of the staves *(above, right)*. Trim the splines flush with the top end of the staves using a flush-cutting saw.

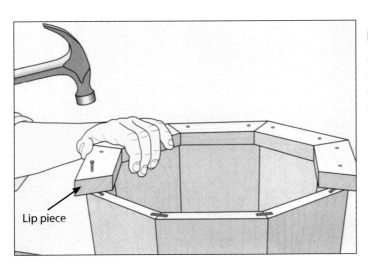

Lip piece

6 **Installing the lip.** Trim the lip pieces to length by mitering each end at 22½°. Apply glue to the contacting surfaces of the staves and lip pieces, and position each piece so its ends align with the seams between the staves. Use two nails to fix each lip piece to its stave *(left)*.

Serving Trolley

Anatomy of a Serving Trolley

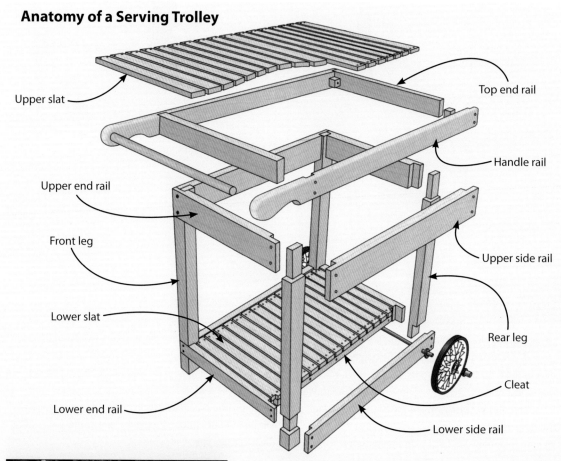

Upper slat

Top end rail

Handle rail

Upper end rail

Front leg

Upper side rail

Lower slat

Rear leg

Cleat

Lower end rail

Lower side rail

The serving trolley rolls on wheels designed as replacements for gas barbecues. With its convenient handle, the trolley is easy to move around, and its stout legs and rails, joined with half-laps, make the piece sturdy and durable.

Cutting List

Item	Qty	Th	W or Diam	L
Top end rails	2	1¼"	2½"	21⅛"
Handle rails	2	1¼"	2½"	47"
Upper slats	18	¾"	1¾"	20⅛"
Upper side rails	2	1¼"	4"	32"
Upper end rails	2	1¼"	4"	20"
Front legs	2	1½"	2½"	27"
Rear legs	2	1½"	2½"	30"
Lower end rails	2	1¼"	2¼"	20"
Lower side rails	2	1¼"	2¼"	32"
Lower slats	15	¾"	1¾"	17½"
Handle	1		1"	21½"
Cleats	2	1¼"	1¼"	30⅝"

Making the Frame

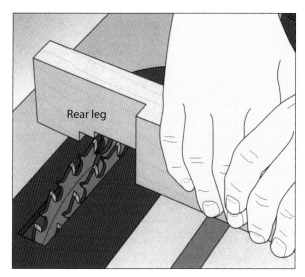

Rear leg

1 **Preparing the stock.** Consisting of the side and end rails, and the legs, the frame of the serving trolley is assembled with half-lap joinery. On your table saw, install a dado head and adjust it to maximum width. Refer to the anatomy illustration opposite for the location and size of the rabbets and dadoes required. At the bottom end of the rear legs, for example, start by cutting a rabbet along the outside face to accept the lower side rail. The length of the rabbet should equal the width of the side rail and its depth should be one-half the stock thickness. Next, cut a rabbet along the outside edge of the leg to accommodate the lower end rail. Position the rip fence so you can feed the stock along the fence as you define the rabbet shoulder, then make a series of passes to remove the remaining waste *(left)*. Guide the workpiece with the miter gauge for each of these passes.

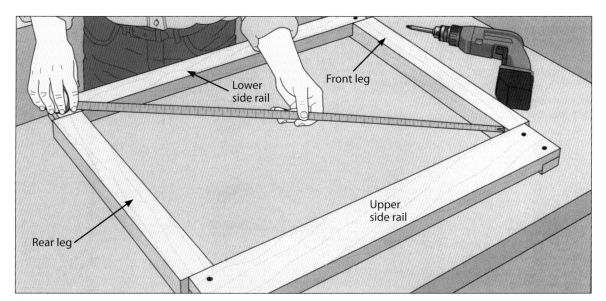

Lower side rail

Front leg

Upper side rail

Rear leg

2 **Fastening the side rails and legs together.** Once all the joinery cuts are made, spread glue on the contacting surfaces of the legs and side rails, and fit the rails and one pair of front and rear legs together. Use two screws to reinforce each joint, driving the fasteners through the rails and into the legs. To check whether the assembly is square, measure the diagonals between opposite corners immediately after tightening the screws *(above)*. The two results should be the same. If not, install a bar clamp across the longer diagonal. Tighten the clamp a little at a time, measuring as you go until the two diagonals are equal.

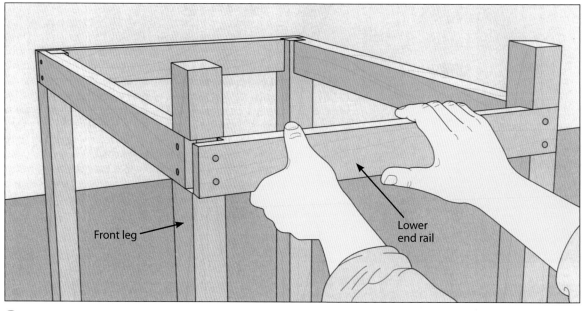

Front leg

Lower
end rail

3 **Installing the end rails.** Once both sides
of the frame are assembled, add the four
end rails. Use glue and screws to fasten the
upper end rails to the legs, then set the assembly
upside down and fix the lower end rails in
position *(above)*.

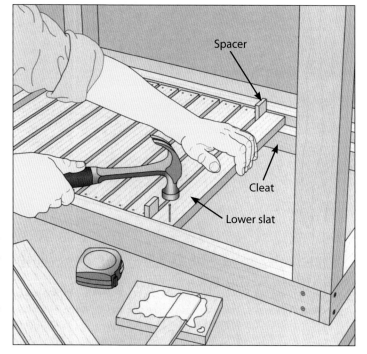

Spacer

Cleat

Lower slat

4 **Installing the lower slats.** Using glue and
screws, attach a cleat along the inside face of
each lower side rail so the top edges of the cleats
are ⅝ inch below the top edges of the rails; apply
only a few drops of adhesive along the length of
the cleat, rather than covering its entire surface to
avoid trapping water between the rails and cleats.
Start installing the slats at one end rail. Notch the
ends of the first and last slats to accommodate
the legs, and fix each piece in place with two nails
at each end. Use ¼-inch spacers to separate the
slats *(right)*.

Attaching the Top

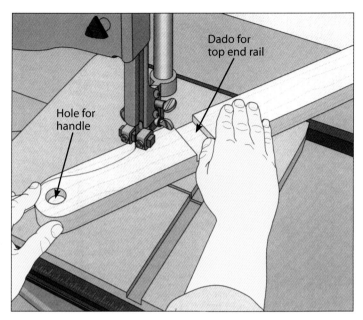

Hole for handle

Dado for top end rail

1 **Preparing the handle rails.** Start by preparing the handle rails for the top end rails and the handle. For the end rails, cut a ½-inch-deep, 1¼-inch-wide dado across the inside face of each handle rail. For the handle, drill a 1-inch-diameter hole as deep as one-half the stock thickness. Next, outline the curve at the front end of the rail and cut it on your band saw *(left)*. Use the rail to outline the curve on the second piece and repeat the cut. Smooth the cut surface with sandpaper or a spindle sander, then round over the outside edges with a router.

2 **Assembling the top frame.** Using glue and screws, fasten the top end rails to one of the handle rails. Glue the handle into its hole, then fit the second handle rail onto the assembly *(below)*, fixing it in place with adhesive and screws.

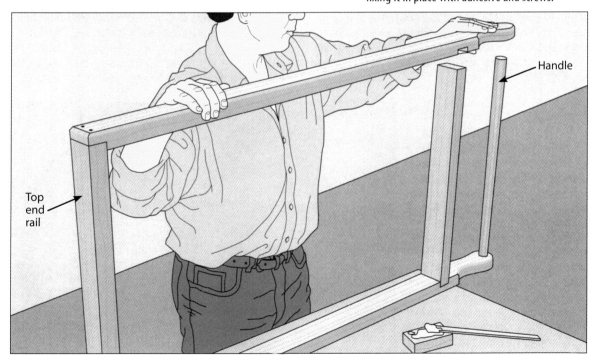

Handle

Top end rail

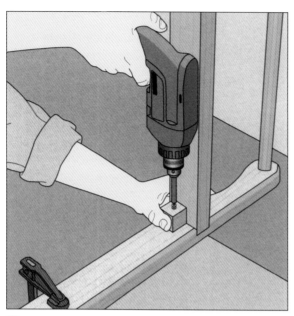

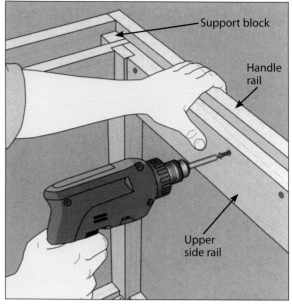

Support block

Handle rail

Upper side rail

3 **Attaching the support blocks.** Cut four 1-inch-square blocks and drill a ⅛-inch-diameter hole through each one. Glued and screwed to the handle rails, the blocks will support the slats at the front and back ends of the top. Clamp the top assembly on edge to a work surface and attach a block to each corner formed by the handle rails and top end rails *(above)*; position the blocks ⅞ inch below the top edge of the rails.

4 **Attaching the top to the upper rails.** Lower the top over the upper rails; it should fit snugly around the outside of the frame. Holding the top so that the top edges of the support blocks and upper rails are flush, fasten the rails together *(above)*. Glue and fasten the top slats in place, as shown on page 130. Use the support blocks and the top of the frame to support the slats in place of the long cleats used in the bottom of the frame. Install the upper slats as you did the lower ones, nailing them to the upper rails and support blocks.

5 **Installing the wheels.** Set the trolley upside down on a work surface and drill a ⅝-inch-diameter hole through each lower rail 3 inches from its end. Make sure the holes are aligned. Slide a ½-inch-diameter axle rod through the holes and slip a washer on each end of the rod. Fit a wheel onto each end of the axle *(right)*, then lock it in place with a second washer and a pressure nut. Tap the nut in place with a hammer, while holding a block of wood against the opposite end of the axle.

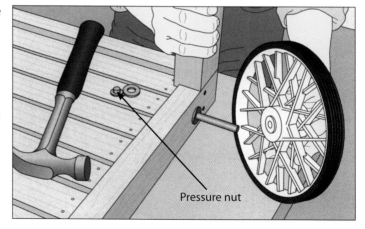

Pressure nut

Garden Arbor

Anatomy of a Garden Arbor

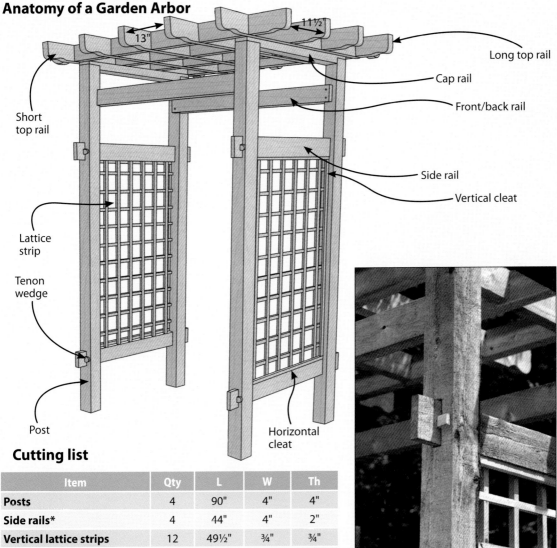

13"

11½"

Long top rail

Cap rail

Front/back rail

Short top rail

Side rail

Vertical cleat

Lattice strip

Tenon wedge

Post

Horizontal cleat

Cutting list

Item	Qty	L	W	Th
Posts	4	90"	4"	4"
Side rails*	4	44"	4"	2"
Vertical lattice strips	12	49½"	¾"	¾"
Horizontal lattice strips	20	30"	¾"	¾"
Cap rails	2	38"	4"	2"
Short top rails	5	60"	4"	2"
Long top rails	4	82"	4"	2"
Vertical cleats	4	49½"	¾"	¾"
Horizontal cleats	4	30"	¾"	¾"
Front/Back rails	2	58"	4"	2"

*Note: Length includes tenon length.

A tusk tenon joint fixes the side rails of the arbor to the posts. The end of the side rail is fitted through a mortise on the post, and a tenon wedge is driven through a hole in the rail, locking the joint. This traditional joinery method complements the rustic look of this unfinished piece, built from northern white cedar.

Making Tusk Tenons

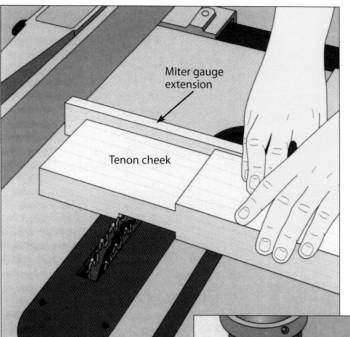

Miter gauge extension

Tenon cheek

1 Roughing the side rails. Start building the arbor by cutting the tusk tenons that join the side rails to the post. To cut the tenons at the ends of the rails on your table saw, install a dado head and adjust it to its maximum width, and attach an extension board to the miter gauge. Set the cutting height at ½ inch and position the rip fence for a 12-inch-wide cut. Feed the rail face down with one end riding along the fence to define the tenon shoulder. Make a series of passes to complete the tenon cheek, then turn the rail over and repeat the process on the other side. Cut tenons at the other end of the rail and at both ends of the remaining rails. Hold the edge of the rail flush against the miter gauge extension for every pass.

2 Roughing out the mortises in the posts. You can cut the post mortises by hand, or use a mortiser or a drill press, fitted with either a mortising attachment or a 1-inch-diameter spade bit, as shown at right. The mortises should start 18 inches from the bottom and 24 inches from the top of the posts. Use the finished tenons to lay out the length and width of the mortises, making sure the outlines are centered on the inside faces of the posts. Then clamp a backup panel to your drill press table and set the post on the panel, centering the outline under the bit. Drill a hole through the post at each end of the outline *(right)*, then bore a series of overlapping holes to complete the mortise.

Post

Mortise outline

Backup panel

3 Cleaning up the mortises. Square the walls of the mortises using a chisel as wide as the mortises. Holding the chisel vertically, bevel facing the waste, align the tip with one of your cutting lines and tap the tool with a wooden mallet *(right)*. Continue around the perimeter of the mortise until all the waste is cleared away. Test-fit each tenon in its mortise and widen or lengthen the cavity as needed.

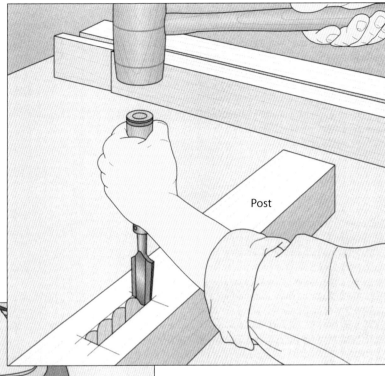

Post

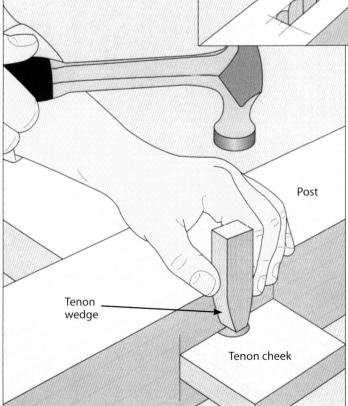

Post

Tenon wedge

Tenon cheek

4 Assembling the posts and rails. Fit the posts and rails together and mark a line along the top of each cheek where the tenon emerges from the mortise. Disassemble the joint and drill a 1-inch-diameter hole through the tenon centered on the line. Cut a ½-by-1-inch hardwood piece into the bullet shape shown at left; make the length of the tenon wedge about equal to the post thickness. Slide the tenon into the mortise and strike the wedge firmly with a hammer until the joint is tight.

1 **Installing the cleats.** Cut the cleats that frame the inside edges of the posts and side rails, mitering both ends of each piece at 45°. Start with the cleats along the rails, nailing the pieces in place, then install the one along the posts. For each cleat, drive the first nail about 2 inches from one end, continuing at about 8-inch intervals. Use a tape measure periodically to check that the cleats are offset by about ⅛ inch from the outside edges of the posts and rails *(right)*.

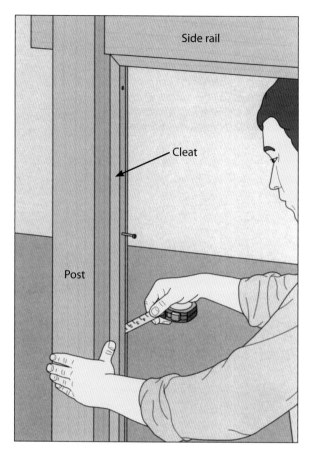

2 **Preparing the lattice strips.** The dadoes for the half-laps joining the lattice strips together can be cut one after another on the table saw using a dado head and a simple jig made from an extension board clamped to the miter gauge. Feed the extension into the blades to cut a dado, then slide the extension along the miter gauge so the space between the dado and the blades equals 4 inches. Screw the extension to the gauge and cut a second dado. Then, insert a tight-fitting wooden key in the first dado so it projects at least 2 inches from the extension. For each lattice strip, butt the edge of the board against the key and hold an edge flush against the extension. Feed the strip into the blades to cut a first dado, then fit the notch you just cut over the key and make a second cut. Continue cutting dadoes in this manner *(below)* until you reach the opposite end of the strip. Hook your thumbs around the extension to steady the strip during each pass.

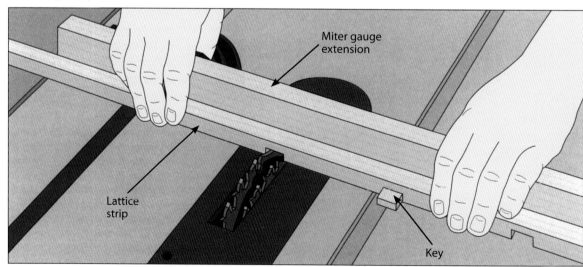

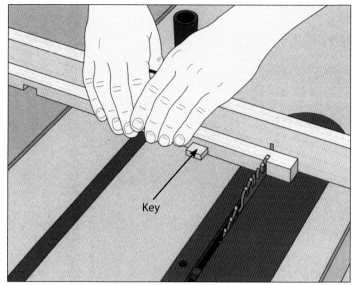

Key

3 Cutting the lattice strips to length.

Once all the joinery cuts have been in the lattice strips, use the same setup to cut the pieces to length. Replace the dado head with a combination blade. For each strip, slip the last dado you cut over the key and feed the piece into the blade *(left)*.

4 Assembling and installing the lattice.

Lay out the horizontal lattice strips on a work surface, spread some glue into all the dadoes and fit the vertical strips in position *(below)*. Use a wooden mallet to close the joints snugly, then reinforce every second joint with a nail. To install the lattice, hold the panel against the inside face of the cleats and fasten the strips to the cleats, driving a screw into each corner and into the center of each side *(inset)*.

5 Attaching the cap rails. Cut a 1-inch-deep rabbet at each end of the cap rails; the rabbets should be as long as the post width. Set a side assembly on a work surface, spread glue on the contacting surfaces and fit the cap rail in position *(right)*. Reinforce each joint with screws.

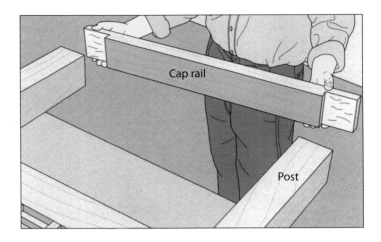

Cap rail

Post

Building the Top

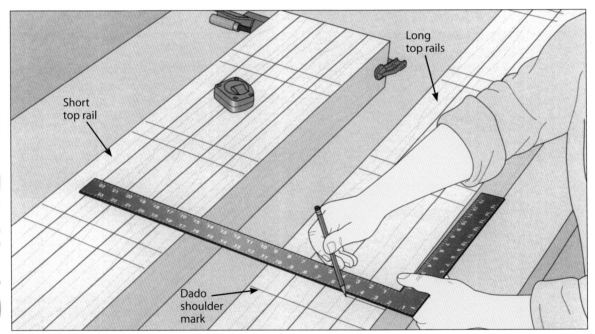

Short top rail

Long top rails

Dado shoulder mark

1 Outlining the half-laps on the top rails. The top rails comprising the top of the arbor are joined with half-lap joints. To mark out the dadoes in all the pieces in a single setup—and ensure that they align—clamp the five short top rails and then the four long top rails together face to face. Make sure the ends

of the pieces in each set align. Starting 14 inches from one end of the boards, begin marking the dado shoulders. To extend the lines accurately across the rails, use a carpenter's square, butting one arm against the outside edge of the stock *(above)*. Each dado should be 2 inches wide. Mark the dado depth—2 inches—on each rail.

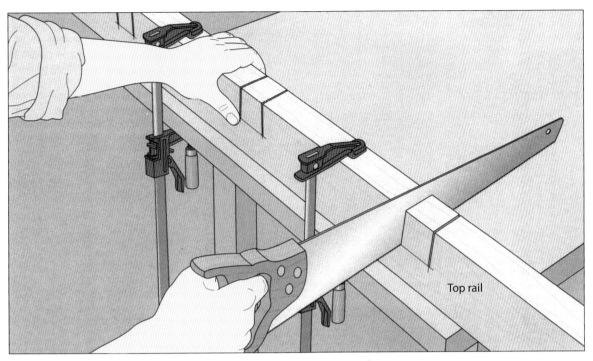

Top rail

2 **Sawing the dado shoulders.** Because the top rails are unwieldy to cut on the table saw, you should make the dadoes by hand. Clamp the workpiece bottom-face up to a work surface and use a crosscut saw to cut along the shoulder lines *(above)*. Stop each kerf at the depth line.

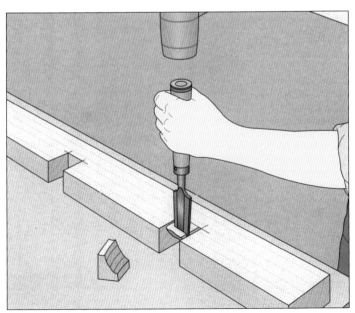

3 **Chiseling out the waste.** Once all the dado shoulders have been cut, turn the workpiece on one side and use a chisel as wide as the dadoes to remove the waste. Starting just below the bottom edge of the stock, hold the chisel vertically, with the bevel facing the bottom edge, and tap the tool with a mallet to sever a piece of waste wood *(left)*. Continue in this fashion until you make a final cut with the chisel tip aligned with the depth line.

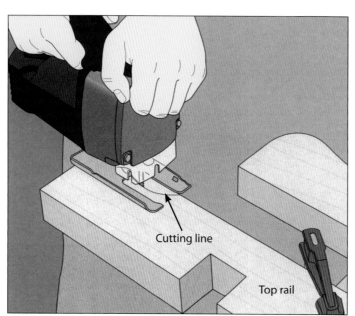

Cutting line

Top rail

4 Shaping the ends of the top rails.

Referring to the anatomy illustration *(page 133)*, draw the decorative curve at the ends of the top rails on a piece of ¼-inch plywood and cut out the profile on your band saw. Using the plywood piece as a template, transfer the curve onto each rail. Clamp the rail to a work surface with the end to be cut extending off the table, and cut the curve with a saber saw *(left)*. Once all the rails have been shaped, sand the cut ends smooth and assemble the pieces with glue and screws as you did the lattice *(page 136)*.

Installing the Arbor

1 Burying the anchors.
The posts of the arbor can be set in concrete or—more easily—metal anchors that are driven into the ground. Place the arbor where it will go and mark the location of the posts. Fit a length of post stock into each anchor and use a sledgehammer to drive the stock and anchor into the ground *(right)*. Continue until the top end of each anchor is near the ground. Make sure the tops of the four anchors are all level. Remove the post stock from the anchors and insert the posts.

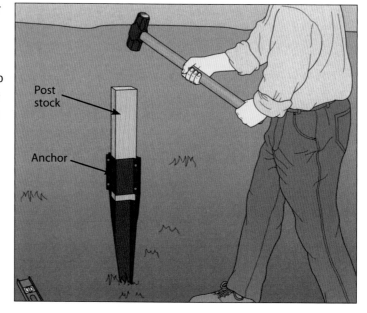

Post stock

Anchor

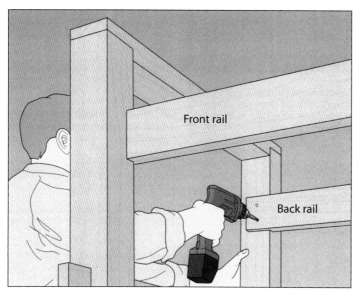

2 Attaching the front and back rails. Cut a 1-inch-deep and 3-inch-long rabbet at each end of the front and back rails. Then fit the rails in place and secure them with two screws at each end *(left)*.

3 Installing the top. To complete building the arbor, work with a helper to lift the top into position *(below)*. If you are using stepladders, make sure they are placed securely on solid ground. Nail the top rails of the arbor to the cap rails.

INDEX

Note: Page numbers in **bold** indicate projects.

More Great Books from Fox Chapel Publishing

Back to **Basics**
Straight Talk for Today's **Woodworker**

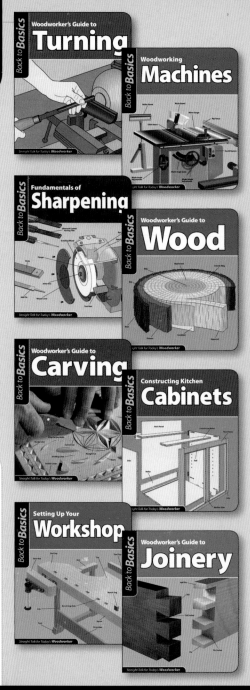

Get *Back to Basics* with the core information you need to succeed.

Woodworker's Guide to Turning
ISBN: 978-1-56523-498-7
$19.95 • 144 Pages

Fundamentals of Sharpening
ISBN: 978-1-56523-496-3
$19.95 • 120 Pages

Woodworker's Guide to Carving
ISBN: 978-1-56523-497-0
$19.95 • 160 Pages

Setting Up Your Workshop
ISBN: 978-1-56523-463-5
$19.95 • 152 Pages

Woodworking Machines
ISBN: 978-1-56523-465-9
$19.95 • 192 Pages

Woodworker's Guide to Wood
ISBN: 978-1-56523-464-2
$19.95 • 160 Pages

Constructing Kitchen Cabinets
ISBN: 978-1-56523-466-6
$19.95 • 144 Pages

Woodworker's Guide to Joinery
ISBN: 978-1-56523-462-8
$19.95 • 192 Pages

Shaker Furniture
12 Timeless Woodworking Projects
By Editors of Skills Institute Press

Discover the timeless projects in the *Built to Last* Series. These are the projects that stand the test of time in function and form, in the techniques they employ, and represent the pieces every woodworker should build in a lifetime.

ISBN: 978-1-56523-467-3
$19.95 • 144 Pages

Look For These Books at Your Local Bookstore or Specialty Retailer
To order direct, call **800-457-9112** or visit *www.FoxChapelPublishing.com*

By mail, please send check or money order + $4.00 per book for S&H to:
Fox Chapel Publishing, 1970 Broad Street, East Petersburg, PA 17520